ECONOMIC AND SOCIAL COMMISSION
FOR ASIA AND THE PACIFIC

STUDIES ON GENDER AND DEVELOPMENT

SOCIAL SAFETY NETS

FOR WOMEN

UNITED NATIONS

New York, 2003

UNITED NATIONS PUBLICATION
Sales No. E.03.II.F.19
Copyright © United Nations 2003
ISBN: 92-1-120158-6

ACKNOWLEDGEMENTS

This publication is based upon papers prepared for the ESCAP Expert Group Meeting on Social Safety Nets for Women held at Bangkok from 2 to 4 May 2001. Chapter I draws upon the regional study prepared by Ms. Hye-Hoon Lee. Chapters II to VII are based upon country papers presented by the following: Mr. Herman Haeruman (Indonesia), Ms. Yeong-Ran Park (Republic of Korea), Mr. Voravidh Charoenlert (Thailand), Ms. Jie Du (China), Ms. Ito Peng (Japan) and Mr. Paguman Singh (Malaysia).

The designations employed and the presentation of the material in this publication do not imply the expression of any opinion whatsoever on the part of the Secretariat of the United Nations concerning the legal status of any country, territory, city or area or of its authorities, or concerning the delimitation of its frontiers or boundaries.

The opinions, figures and estimates set forth in this publication are the responsibility of the authors, and should not necessarily be considered as reflecting the views or carrying the endorsement of the United Nations.

On 1 July 1997, Hong Kong became Hong Kong, China. Mention of "Hong Kong" in the text refers to a date prior to 1 July 1997.

On 20 December 1999, Macau became Macao, China, Mention of "Macau" in the text refers to a date prior to 20 December 1999.

Mention of firm names and commercial products does not imply the endorsement of the United Nations.

This publication has been issued without formal editing.

PREFACE

Governments in the region relied, to a large extent, upon economic growth to reduce the incidence of poverty in their countries and ensure social security for all. This approach brought dramatic success for a number of countries, in their efforts at poverty alleviation. While this developmental thrust is understandable, in that the governments of the market economies were attempting to move their countries into a positive condition of development, it also left these countries particularly vulnerable. An acute economic contraction, such as that brought on by the financial crisis of 1997/1998, was enough to undo much of the progress in poverty eradication achieved over decades of development.

The social impact of the financial crisis was evident in several ways. First, the financial shocks caused currency depreciation that produced changes in relative prices, which in turn changed relative wages, employment patterns and consumption baskets. Additionally, these price increases primarily affected goods that were imported, such as pharmaceuticals, food and fuel. And these price increases particularly affected the urban poor, who are net consumers. Open unemployment, and increasing underemployment initially affected the urban areas which were the major areas of factory employment for the rapidly growing export industries and the construction industry. There was also a reduction in demand for international labour which affected countries that rely on this source of labour for a large proportion of international exchange. In some cases there was loss of assets in the form of savings, some possessions, or even houses serviced by short-term mortgages. This particularly affected the lower middle class in the urban areas. The poor were particularly affected by inflation because they typically hold more of any savings they may have in the form of money, which was losing its purchasing power. The sharp rise in credit rates reduced consumption and housing construction. The inability to raise credit led to factory closures and unemployment.

Report after report that followed the crisis, however, indicated that women were often the first workers to be laid off – both because the industries in which they predominate (e.g. textiles and garments) were those most affected by the crisis and because women were less unionised and therefore easier to sack. The unemployment situation was also aggravated by increasing numbers of returning migrant labourers, many of whom were women, who were being expelled by countries which were experiencing their own unemployment problems. Moreover, cuts in public social sector expenditure, that came in the aftermath of the crisis, rising prices for foodstuffs and other basic commodities caused partly by increasing costs of imports brought even more hardships, especially for women who have primary responsibility for balancing household budgets and care of the family.

In response to these social impacts of the crisis, many women moved into alternative forms of self-employment in the informal sector, but they often lacked the necessary technical skills to do so and faced difficulties in gaining access to training or to credit. Many therefore were forced to settle for easy entry activities such as petty trading or the sex industry but these jobs generate very little returns or expose them to new risks. Increasingly, retrenched women's newfound jobs were those characterised by lowpay, job insecurity, casual employment and lack of benefits.

The main lessons of the crisis, in terms of social development, are threefold. First, the crisis had a large, negative effect on household welfare, mainly due to labour demand shocks. Poverty became more acute throughout the region, and other social indicators, such as decent work, school attendance, healthcare and others took a turn for the worse in some countries. Second, households and governments largely reacted to the crisis in sensible ways. Households protected their consumption of some critical items, such as staple foods, while the labour market reflected the impact of falling wage incomes and the reduced availability of formal sector jobs Governments launched emergency efforts, most often funded by donor organizations to provide urgently needed financial support and modified existing safety net programmes, and worked hard to gather data which could be used to inform policies. Additionally, informal social protection mechanisms provided by the family, community and non-governmental organizations (NGOs), were also mobilised to mitigate the shocks of the crisis. These measures, however, were not sufficient to adequately address the problems and hardships brought about by the aggregate shocks of an economic crisis. The third lesson, therefore, was that the crisis exposed important limitations in the ability of private and public safety nets to cope with a shock of this magnitude, and revealed the need for more comprehensive social protection policies and institutions to help households manage risks.

The social protection schemes existing in the crisis-hit countries, prior to the crisis, provide protection for formal sector workers but only to a very limited extent. Formal statutory social protection programmes such as old age and disability benefits, pension systems, etc. were limited in their coverage and does not include the self-employed, the part-time employed, daily labourers in urban centres who come from rural areas, laid off workers from state owned enterprises (in the case of China), agricultural labourers, domestic workers, migrant workers and those working in the informal sector. Importantly, women are concentrated in many of these sectors of employment, more so in the informal sector. What emerged from reviews of the pre-crisis social protection schemes as well as the crisis-initiated social safety nets, was that these policies and programmes were lacking in gender responsiveness.

There is ample evidence from several studies and reports that women play a major role in managing the response to economic shocks at the household and often the community level. It is they who have to make the decisions, such as food expenditures, on which the survival of the household is based. At times of crisis they are also often active in strategizing to increase household income, such as joining the informal sector by selling goods. Gender-blind employment and income-generation programmes can unwittingly disadvantage women. Major priority must therefore be given to programmes that can be delivered to this segment of societies.

This study examines the social protection systems and, particularly, the crisis-designed social safety nets in a selected number of countries. A primary question in this study is whether the initiatives, to mitigate the shocks of the crisis, adequately reflect the different circumstances of women and men in the labour force, particularly, and society in general. Specifically, did the programmes attempt to specifically target the disadvantaged women? Did government budgets specifically target women as recipients of social safety net programmes? What role did women play in informal social safety nets activities?

The social costs of the crisis were concentrated in Indonesia, the Republic of Korea and Thailand and to lesser extents, other countries in the region. As such, the focus of the country studies is on the situation of women in these countries. Three other countries were selected for this study, China, Japan and Malaysia. Although China managed to escape the most severe impacts of the crisis, the economy and peoples were nonetheless affected. Moreover, the country was, and still is, undergoing a structural adjustment process that requires serious consideration on social protection systems. Japan has an established social protection system; it was chosen as a comparative study. The case of Malaysia is also different, being hit by the crisis but took a somewhat different path in responding to the shocks of the crisis.

The structure of this study reflects the countries selected. Chapter I serves as an overview and Chapters II to VII examine the situations in the selected countries. The study ends with a set of recommendations flowing from the previous chapters. These recommendations are taken from the Report of the Expert Group Meeting on Social Safety Nets for Women, organized by the Economic and Social Commission for Asia and the Pacific, from 2 to 4 May 2001 in Bangkok.

The crisis has now abated to varying extents, but effects of the social costs incurred have not completely disappeared. A key challenge remains, i.e. to identify effective policy instruments that could be adopted in short-term safety net rescue operations as well as long-term comprehensive social protection that will reflect the particular features of hardships as differentiated between men and women. In other words, if social protection and social safety net policies and programmes are to be effective, they will have to reflect the social and economic conditions of both women and men in the societies concerned.

It is hoped that this study will benefit policy makers, planners, administrators, academics and others in formulating and implementing effective, gender-responsive and sustainable social protection systems and social safety nets to ensure that workers and families can deal with future economic downturns.

The generous funding support of the Government of the Netherlands for the implementation of the project is gratefully acknowledged.

CONTENTS

CONTENTS *(continued)*

TABLES

TABLES *(continued)*

FIGURE

CHAPTER I.

THE SITUATION OF WOMEN IN THE ASIAN
AND PACIFIC REGION

In 1999, ESCAP launched a project, entitled "Evaluation of Income and Employment Generating Programmes for Alleviating Socio-economic Impacts of the Economic Crisis". This project was aimed at evaluating various government policies and programmes implemented to alleviate the socio-economic costs of rising unemployment and loss of income associated with the Asian economic crisis. The focus of the research was on the experiences in the three hardest hit countries viz. Indonesia, the Republic of Korea, and Thailand.

The research project involved surveys and in-depth analyses at institutional and beneficiary levels to assess the effectiveness of four income and employment generating programmes: public works, unemployment insurance schemes, microcredit, and credit for small and medium-sized enterprises (SMEs). The main objectives of the project were to (i) assess the overall success or failure of the programmes in terms of institutional goals and objectives and (ii) evaluate the target efficiency of the programmes.

This particular monograph formed a part of the larger aforementioned project. The main objectives of this study are to identify and evaluate whether or not gender issues were attended to in the design and implementation of the social safety net policies and programmes. In other words, if safety net policies are to be effective, they will have to reflect the social and economic conditions of women in these societies. This study seeks to identify the strengths and weaknesses of each programme in the countries concerned in order to devise more effective policy responses and actions that would strengthen the social protection system with more equal emphasis between women and men.

Chapter I will begin with a review of women's status in the region, followed by an overview of the Asian economic crisis and its social impacts, especially on women. This chapter will also provide an overview of the various policy measures, initiated by governments in response to the crisis, and their effectiveness in gender terms. The following chapters will examine, country by country, the context and rationale of the programmes, their strengths and weaknesses and their impact in addressing the problems faced by women. The social costs of the economic crisis were concentrated in Indonesia, the Republic of Korea and Thailand and, to lesser extents, other countries and areas in the region. As such, Chapters II, III and IV will look at the situations in Indonesia, the Republic of Korea and Thailand respectively. In Chapters V, VI and VII the experiences in China, Japan and Malaysia will be examined. The study will conclude, in the Annex, with some policy implications flowing from the previous chapters. These policy recommendations were the result of deliberations, on these country reports, at the ESCAP Expert Group Meeting on Social Safety Nets for Women held from 2 to 4 May 2001.

A. Women in Asia

Since the Fourth World Conference on Women in 1995 at which the Beijing Declaration and the Platform for Action was adopted, significant progress has been made in a number of areas of concern for women in the region. There has been success in increasing female literacy and life expectancy rates, and reducing maternal mortality rates. In employment, there has been a marked improvement in female labour force participation, with gender differentials in wages falling in many instances. An increasing number of women in Asia and the Pacific are enabled to participate in the economy because of policies that provide skills training in new technologies, support for self-employed women in small and medium-scale industries, childcare services, etc. Additionally, violence against women has become illegal in a number of countries. Improvements in law enforcement and greater allocation of resources to violence prevention, protection and rehabilitation services for women, have all contributed to significant achievements in addressing violence against women. New health strategies have also been introduced for women and infants and there is a greater understanding of the gender dimensions of the human immunodeficiency virus (HIV) and acquired immunodeficiency syndrome (AIDS). More countries now have separate national plans for women and the machineries to implement these plans.

However, many and new challenges are apparent, not least of which are those posed by the process of globalization, the recent economic crisis and long-standing sociocultural attitudes and institutional practices biased against women. Globalization has enhanced employment opportunities for women but in times of economic slowdown, women are often the first to be retrenched and forced to fall back on the informal and rural sectors for survival. Despite improved or new pro-women legislation in several countries, there is an increasing number of women trafficked for sexual exploitation and forced labour, with growing incidents of other forms of violence against women. Although significant progress has been made in alleviating poverty in the region, women in poverty continue to suffer from economic hardship and social exclusion. Additionally, with the changing demographic structure of the region and increase in the proportion of older persons, especially older women, the need for appropriate policies and systems to provide economic and social support will be important issues. Promoting the greater participation of women in decision-making will continue to be a formidable challenge. The task of social and economic empowerment of women therefore remains a priority area of concern for the countries of the region.

1. Demographic trends and dynamics

In most Asian countries, the relationship between women and men is punctuated with glaring inequalities, and concerns about this situation are reflected in the countries selected for this study. One effect of gender inequality in many Asian countries is the low ratio of females to males. While the worldwide ratio of women to men is 98.5 to 100, in the Asian region it is 95.7 to 100 (ESCAP 2002).

Looking at subregions, the East and North-East Asian regions, in contrast to South-East Asia, shows a stable and low female to male sex ratio (table I.1). As for the particular countries considered in this study, the Republic of Korea has a very stable and low female sex ratio of 98.4 females to 100 males on average. Table I.2 shows that the country has a very low female to male sex ratios among infants, while that of the elderly over 65 is unusually high. This indicates that the higher sex ratios among the elderly raise the female sex ratios of all ages and thereby distortions of sex ratios at birth will be greater than the figures imply.

As for the other two countries in this study, Indonesia shows a slightly decreasing and higher female sex ratio of 100.4 females to 100 males. In Thailand there is a steady upward movement in the sex ratio, at 100.5 females to 100 males.

These figures show, as has previous research, that there is a great variation among countries with regard to the existence of sex preference for children. A discrepancy in sex ratios across the region mainly indicates societal differences in preference for males over females.

Gender preference for children of a certain sex can have an impact not only on fertility but also on mortality. There is evidence that advanced medical technologies such as those used for pre-natal sex identification have been exploited as a tool for the selection of children by the sex of the fetus. In other words, ultrasound and amniocentesis have been used as methods for determining whether or not to abort a fetus. In general, a preference for children of one sex, i.e. males, may lead to problems of sex discrimination, sex-selective abortion, female infanticide, a poor quality of life for females, deterioration of the family system and have effects on the future fertility of countries; it may even interrupt the advance towards sustainable social and economic development in countries where such a preference exists.

Table I.1. Female sex ratios in the Asian region

(unit: per 100 males)

Subregion/country	1985	1990	1995	1998	2000
East and North-East Asia	95.2	95.0	95.2	95.3	95.4
South-East Asia	101.2	100.8	100.5	100.4	100.4
Republic of Korea	98.3	98.8	98.5	98.3	98.3
Indonesia	100.9	100.6	100.5	100.4	100.4
Thailand	99.5	99.7	100.0	100.2	100.5

Source: ESCAP, *Statistics on Women in Asia and the Pacific 1999* (ST/ESCAP/1995).

Table I.2. Age-specific female sex ratios in the Asian region

(unit: per 100 males)

Subregion/country	All ages	0-4	5-14	15-24	25-34	35-49	50-64	65+
East and North-East Asia								
1985	95.2	92.9	94.0	93.8	93.7	91.3	95.9	128.5
1990	95.0	90.6	92.9	95.5	93.6	92.5	93.7	125.7
1995	95.2	89.9	91.5	94.3	95.4	93.2	94.0	124.2
2000	95.4	90.1	90.4	93.2	95.5	94.5	94.7	122.7

(continued)

Table I.2 *(continued)*

(unit: per 100 males)

Subregion/country	All ages	0-4	5-14	15-24	25-34	35-49	50-64	65+
South-East Asia								
1985	101.2	96.9	96.9	99.4	103.2	105.2	108.3	123.1
1990	100.8	96.1	97.2	97.8	102.1	104.0	108.3	124.8
1995	100.5	95.7	96.6	97.5	100.0	104.0	109.2	125.0
2000	100.4	95.9	96.1	97.4	98.3	103.6	108.6	126.8
Republic of Korea								
1985	98.3	91.4	92.5	92.1	97.7	96.0	116.5	164.5
1990	98.8	89.3	93.6	94.4	96.1	95.0	111.8	165.3
1995	98.5	87.1	91.5	94.2	95.7	96.3	106.5	169.1
2000	98.3	87.1	88.2	93.8	95.1	97.1	103.5	164.5
Indonesia								
1985	100.9	97.1	97.5	99.7	101.9	105.4	105.1	116.9
1990	100.6	96.9	97.4	98.2	101.6	104.3	106.5	115.2
1995	100.5	96.4	97.3	97.6	100.2	103.4	108.5	116.2
2000	100.4	96.3	96.9	97.7	98.7	102.8	108.4	120.1
Thailand								
1985	99.5	95.9	96.2	96.5	100.0	101.3	106.9	128.5
1990	99.7	96.4	96.4	96.3	98.6	100.9	108.4	127.6
1995	100.0	96.3	96.4	96.7	97.2	101.4	108.0	127.9
2000	100.5	96.4	96.6	96.7	97.1	101.4	107.4	130.7

Source: ESCAP, *Statistics on Women in Asia and the Pacific 1999* (ST/ESCAP/1995).

Another demographic trend of concern is the falling fertility rates in the region, especially the wealthier Asian countries. Fourteen countries and cities in Asia have fertility rates below the 2.1 births per woman required to replace the older generations. This is more pronounced in the region's more affluent countries and areas, such as Hong Kong, China, Japan, Republic of Korea and Singapore where fertility rates are below 1.5 per woman, while Thailand is marginally higher at 1.8. Women in these countries are having fewer babies or no children at all because of career pressures.

Asia's fertility rate plunged from around six children per woman from 1950-1955 to 2.7 children per woman between 1995-2000. The current fertility rate in the region of 2.7 children per woman is slightly below the world average. The implications are far-reaching and profound, as they affect the age structure of the population, giving rise to population ageing, labour force shortages, increased elderly dependency ratios and feminization of the elderly population.

One key impact will be on the labour force, where there will be fewer younger people to take over jobs left by the greying generation, who may have to work longer than normal before retiring. By 2050, Japan's old-age population – categorised as people aged 65 and above – is forecast to be more than 36 per cent of the total population, up from 17 per cent in

2000. This will be three times as high as the proportion of people aged between 15-64. The proportion of the old-age population will exceed that of the younger population in Singapore by 2020, 2025 in the Republic of Korea, 2035 in China and 2040 in Thailand. What this means is that countries with high social security coverage will come under pressure to provide pensions for the growing number of elderly.

The problem of care for the elderly is likely to be especially acute for older women, who constitute the majority of the elderly in virtually all low-mortality populations. Because of women's greater longevity in most countries of Asia and the tendency for men to marry women younger than themselves, women are more likely than men to end their lives as widows. The implication of this is a serious gender asymmetry in the support and care of the elderly.

Population ageing is also a women's issue in that the care for the elderly is still considered to be the responsibility of the family, part of a cultural value of filial piety. Women in the family or in the community have to play a major role in providing this care and support.

The onset of physical disability in old age may produce a need for support as well as for care if the individual's income depends on continued employment. Likewise, the social disabilities created by a sex-based division of labour or by arbitrary rules of retirement may also create both support and care needs in old age. An important issue in formulating policy, then, is whether social norms concerning such issues as the gender-based division of labour or the mandatory retirement age, create or exacerbate problems for populations as they age. The problems that elderly women face are, moreover, frequently compounded by their difficulties in obtaining sufficient income because of their limited access to pensions and rights to property.

In Asia the numbers of rural elderly are projected to increase in absolute terms. Such increases have implications for health needs and other necessary services. Many countries in the region will face an important elderly dependency ratio, which raises the issue of the possible future vulnerability of the rural elderly as a group in view of the pressures which will be placed on the family and community institutions. A large percentage of the future rural elderly will not benefit from any significant pension, health insurance or social security support which, insofar as they are being developed, are limited mostly to urban elderly. Again, the sex ratio is in favour of women, particularly in rural areas. From a rural-gender perspective, distribution issues such as land property or tenure and other assets need to be examined.

The important point to note is that from a development perspective, due to the declines in fertility, either ongoing or projected, in developing countries, the total dependency ratios will decline slightly for rural populations. The increasing rural elderly dependency ratio is more than compensated by the decline in the children dependency ratio. Such changes can open opportunities in policies and programmes to accelerate development, and also to improve the quality of life of the rural populations. For example, the significant projected declines in the upcoming young generations combined with the stabilization of the adult ones in the region should reduce the purely demographic component of the pressures on land.

However, it should be kept in mind that old-age dependency is more expensive than child dependency.

2. Educational status

In terms of literacy rates, gender gaps across the region appear to be narrowing, although the rate of change is still slow in several countries. There are also subregional variations, with a number of countries in South Asia falling far behind East and South-East Asia in terms of adult female literacy rates. The changes in adult female literacy rates tend to be closely correlated with the outside-home work participation of women. Efforts to reduce gender inequality in education can therefore affect the paid employment of women with the greater likelihood of households investing more in the education of girls.

Looking specifically at the three countries in question, it appears that females are, generally, suffering from lack of adequate educational opportunities (tables I.3 and I.4).

Table I.3. Illiterate population by sex, 15 years and older, Indonesia, Republic of Korea and Thailand, 1985-1995

(unit: per cent)

Country	Year	Females	Males	Total
Republic of Korea	1985	9.9	2.6	6.3
	1990	4.8	1.0	2.9
	1995	3.3	0.7	2.0
Indonesia	1985	42.3	22.5	32.6
	1990	24.7	11.7	18.3
	1995	22.0	10.4	16.3
Thailand	1985	16.0	7.7	11.9
	1990	8.8	4.4	6.6
	1995	8.4	4.0	6.2

Source: ESCAP, *Statistics on Women in Asia and the Pacific 1999* (ST/ESCAP/1995).

Table I.4. Gross enrolment ratios by sex and level of education, Indonesia, Republic of Korea and Thailand

(unit: per cent)

Country	Year	Pre-Primary			First Level			Second Level			Third Level		
		F	M	F-M	F	M	F-M	F	M	F-M	F	M	F-M
Republic of Korea	1985	41	43	−2	98	96	2	91	93	−2	21	46	−25
	1990	55	56	−1	105	105	0	88	91	−3	25	51	−26
	1995	85	85	0	96	95	1	101	101	0	38	66	−28
Indonesia	1985	..	..	..	114	120	−6	..	..	..	4	9	−4
	1990	..	..	..	114	117	−3	40	48	−8	..	..	..
	1994	19	18	1	112	117	−5	44	52	−8	9	14	−5
Thailand	1990	44	43	1	99	100	−1	30	31	−1	..	..	..

Source: ESCAP, *Statistics on Women in Asia and the Pacific 1999* (ST/ESCAP/1995).

Table I.3 summarizes the illiteracy ratios of the three countries by sex. The Republic of Korea has a relatively low female illiteracy of 3.3 per cent, in contrast to Indonesia where it is at 22 per cent and Thailand 8.8 per cent. Despite the variations among these countries, the gender gap in illiteracy is clear. Female illiteracy ratios are 2 to 5 times higher than those for males in the three countries.

Illiteracy can be a crucial obstacle to receiving employment or income support particularly when the process requires written applications or reading written materials. Illiteracy often hinders potential beneficiaries from accessing relevant services and information that social programmes offer.

Table I.4 shows the gender inequality in educational opportunities. The gross enrolment rates at lower levels of education do not reveal significant gender gaps in the countries concerned. The discrepancies are clearer, however, at higher levels of education. The average education of females is low in both Indonesia and Thailand, in contrast to the Republic of Korea where almost all females are reported to advance to secondary education. In Indonesia and Thailand, less than half of females advance to secondary education.

Secondary education in table I.4 includes all types of schools that provide general and/ or specialized instruction, following from at least four years of prior primary education. Schools that fall in this category are middle-level schools, secondary schools, high schools, teacher training colleges, and vocational or technical institutes.

In the case of the Republic of Korea, there is no clear gender disparity up until the third level of education. At the third level, male enrolees almost double that of females. Only 38 per cent of females advance to the third level of education, compared to 66 per cent of males. Indonesia presents a very low level of enrolment ratio for the third level of education for both men and women, but substantial difference across sex is observed and only 9 per cent of females advance to the highest level of education.

3. Labour market status

Labour market participation is one indicator of women's status in the economy. However, women's economic position compared to men's depends on (1) their labour force participation in the wage-earning sector, (2) their occupational attainment, (3) their relative wage level and (4) the time they spend working at home, which reduces the time they can spend in paid employment (Mincer 1962; Becker 1965; Gronau 1980). Home production is a very important element of women's economic activity and an important aspect of women's relative economic position.

The most significant improvement in women's status in the region over the past two decades has been in economic participation. Female labour-force participation rates increased across all the countries in the region for the period of the 1980s and 1990s. The rates of increase have been, in fact, higher than that of male labour-force participation during the same period. This may imply that the increase in female participation reflects the overall expansion of the labour force, driven by rapid economic growth in this region. Nevertheless, the proportionate increase in female participation does indicate an improvement for women, given the past pattern of skewed gender distribution of labour.

It is now widely recognized that women contributed enormously to the dynamic growth in the region. Their productive contributions included their salaried labour in export-related activities and in services, the remittances of migrant women workers, and especially the vast amounts of unpaid, mainly domestic, labour. The female share of total employment by sector in a number of Asian countries was quite high, including the countries considered in this study. Export-oriented production for the world market and the ability to preserve competitiveness in such production over an extended period of time appear to be crucial in explaining women's high share in total employment.

The relationship between the degree of economic development and female share of non-agricultural activity presented may well be explained by the fact that economic development has been export-oriented in most Asian countries. This development strategy relies heavily on rapid growth of low-wage female employment. As Standing (1989) correctly pointed out:

> *Indeed, no country has successfully industrialized or pursued this development strategy without relying on a huge expansion of female labour. And in export processing zones of many industrialising countries it is not uncommon for three-quarters of all workers to be women. The reasons are well known. Much of the assembling and production line work is semi-skilled and low paid; young women, particularly in the newly industrialized countries in Asia, have been socially and economically oppressed for so long that they have low "aspiration wages" and "low efficiency" wages. They are prepared to work for low wages for long workweeks, normally without agitating to join unions, and when their productivity declined after a few years of youthful diligence new cohorts replace them.*

Comparing the three countries in question, Indonesia shows a more drastic increase in female participation compared to the Republic of Korea. The female activity rate in Indonesia grew from 27.7 per cent in 1980 to 38.3 per cent in 1998, while the men's labour activity rate rose moderately from 51.5 per cent to 56.9 per cent over the same period. Despite the remarkable increase, however, female labour activity falls far behind that of males by 18.6 percentage points.

Among the three countries, the female participation rate is the highest in Thailand, 55.7 per cent in 1998 with a 9-percentage point difference with male participation. Strikingly, the gender discrepancy in participation rates in Thailand rose from 5.2 percentage points in 1980 to 9.0 percentage points in 1998. What this says is that, during this period, gender equality in the labour market had not improved in Thailand.

Table I.5. Labour force and participation rates by sex

(unit: per cent)

Subregion/country	Labour Force		Participation Rate		Proportion of Female Labour Force
	Female	Male	Female	Male	
East and North-East Asia	388 499	475 365	53.9	63.5	45
South-East Asia	105 515	141 087	41.9	56.3	43
Republic of Korea	9 511	13 709	41.6	59.0	41
Indonesia	39 601	58 522	38.3	56.9	40
Thailand	16 802	19 462	55.7	64.6	46

Source: ESCAP, *Statistics on Women in Asia and the Pacific 1999* (ST/ESCAP/1995).

In the region as a whole, gender-based wage differentials have been decreasing in several countries, thereby contributing towards more gender equality in the economic field (Ghosh 1999). Available evidence suggests that female wages as a proportion of male wages in manufacturing have been going up. Thus, in the decade between 1987 and 1996, some decline in gender-based wage differentials is evident for Malaysia, the Republic of Korea, Singapore and Thailand.

However, there still remains a discrepancy in wages between males and females as shown in table I.6. In the Republic of Korea, female workers in the manufacturing sector, on average, received only half of the male workers' wage. Thailand is most advanced in terms of wage differences compared to the Republic of Korea. Wages of women workers is three-fourths that of male workers. Looking at a broader range of countries, it appears that women in Japan and the Republic of Korea earn the least relative to their male counterparts, whereas women in China seem to have the highest relative earnings. Some surveys also indicate that women in Viet Nam earned about 72 per cent of the respective male rate of pay in 1992 (Desai 1995) and highly-educated women in Indonesia earned 88 to 90 per cent of the comparable male rate while low-educated women earned 70 to 75 per cent of the associated pay rate for men in 1992 (Manning 1996).

Differences in work position and length of service will affect the gender wage gap. On average, the work position of female workers is inferior to that of male workers and is thus responsible for a substantial part of the observed wage difference. In the Republic of Korea, for example, where a seniority-based wage scheme is practised, female labour is paid less because of women's shorter average working periods.

Although there are a number of theoretical reasons to explain the observed wage discrepancy across genders, the hypothesis that a gender bias exists in the labour market in Asia can still be proved. The inferior work position of females and the corresponding shorter length of service may be the result of a gender bias prevalent in the labour market such as the "glass ceiling" of female employees. There is no concrete evidence that the productivity of female labour is lower than that of its male counterpart. Even in cases where there may be such evidence, it can be a result of gender bias itself exercised against female workers in the labour market.

**Table I.6. Ratio of female to male workers in the manufacturing sector,
Republic of Korea and Thailand, 1990-1995**

(unit: per cent)

Country	*1990*	*1995*
Republic of Korea	50	54
Thailand	64	71

Source: ESCAP, *Statistics on Women in Asia and the Pacific 1999* (ST/ESCAP/1995).
Note: Data for Indonesia not available.

In the informal and rural sectors, government policies play a minimal role or none at all in gender wage differentials. Thus, traditional gender bias can affect both gender-occupational-attainment and wage-determination patterns. This cultural influence normally affects employers and employees, including females. Economic theory suggests that competition will eventually drive from the market employers who discriminate against female employees because they will have to pay higher labour costs than their non-discriminating counterparts. Hence, in a competitive market, gender discrimination is unsustainable (see Krueger 1963; Gordon and Morton 1974; Madden 1975). However, when both employers and employees (including females) share the same biased attitude toward female employees, employers who do not discriminate will be unable to benefit from cheaper female labour. Therefore large, persistent wage discrimination may exist.

Another serious problem causing gender-wage discrimination in developing countries is extensive unemployment in rural and urban areas. The pools of unemployed in less-developed countries encourage, by and large, gender discrimination since so many women are willing to work under discriminatory conditions. As the World Bank pointed out:

Women in developing countries are often over-represented in the informal sector and are so eager for jobs in the modern sector that they willingly ignore employer's failure to implement government-legislated standards.

Much literature argues that the recent trends of privatisation and public-spending cutbacks have severe implications for women not only because women's wages and employment conditions are better on average in the public sector than in the private sector, but also because wage differentials between men and women are smaller in the public sector (Standing 1989).

B. The Asian crisis and its impact on women

The Asian financial crisis formally erupted in April 1997 with the depreciation of the Thai baht triggering a contagion effect on the currencies of Indonesia, the Republic of Korea, Malaysia and Philippines. This soon led to a region-wide economic contraction that saw the gross domestic product (GDP) country after country crashing down one. Indonesia, the fourth most populous country in the world, and the Republic of Korea, the world's eleventh largest economy, were engulfed in the crisis. Inflation pressurized consumer price indexes and reduced real incomes, unemployment rates went up, poverty incidence increased, and income inequality widened (Knowles and others 1999).

Real GDP growth rates of Thailand, the first country to be hit by the crisis, recorded – 0.4 per cent in 1997 and – 8.0 per cent in 1998, respectively. It was a drastic downturn from 8.8 per cent in 1995 and 5.5 per cent in 1996. Indonesia, perhaps the most affected by the crisis, saw a jump of 60 per cent in the consumer price index; a fall of 24 per cent in real per capita income; a 15.9 per cent decline in employment in the construction sector and 9.8 decline in employment in the manufacturing sector; and an increase in poverty incidence from 11 per cent in 1996-97 to 24 per cent in 1998-99. The Republic of Korea, joined the affected group in late 1997, recording – 6.7 per cent growth compared to an earlier decade of an average annual growth of over 7 per cent.

The contagion later on affected the currencies of Brazil; Hong Kong, China; the Russian Federation; and Venezuela where currency devaluation and especially in the case of Russia, capital flight were experienced as well. For many, the Asian crisis has indeed turned into a global crisis of present-day trade and finance globalization where unanticipated and uncontrolled volatility can trigger serious instability and widespread suffering.

1. The social cost of the crisis

Prior to the crisis, Asian countries enjoyed high growth, low unemployment rates, relatively equal income distribution, and low crime rates. The social impacts of the crisis – such as rising unemployment and income inequality – have, therefore been felt painfully in Asia and has led to adverse social consequences.

One major impact of the crisis was the rapid increase in unemployment as hundreds of small and large firms across the region were forced to close their doors. Without exception, unemployment rates increased in all countries (Knowles and others Pernia and Racelis 1999) and where data was available, underemployment, employment of children, and employment in the services and informal sectors were found to increase as well (Lim 1999, Kamoltrakul 1999). The unemployment situation was aggravated by increasing numbers of returning migrant labourers who were expelled by countries struggling with their own unemployment problems. It is estimated that there was, in that period, an excess of 7 million migrant workers in Asia. Reports indicated that Thailand had sent back 800,000 Burmese migrants workers and Malaysia one million workers to Bangladesh and the Philippines. In most cases, unemployment was immediate and without compensation causing obvious distress for workers and their families.

Wage levels recorded sharp declines in most countries in Asia in contrast to years of continuous wage growth for several decades. The Republic of Korea saw its first decline in nominal wages since data on wages had begun to be officially collected. The average wage across all industries declined with the growth rate – 2.5 per cent in 1998, a drastic reduction compared to the pre-crisis level of 7.0 per cent in 1997 and 11.9 per cent in 1996. In Thailand, the loss of real income per income earner reached 21 per cent by the wet season of 1998, declining further from the fall of 17 per cent in the previous dry season.

Unemployment in the Republic of Korea rose drastically to 5.6 per cent in 1998 from 2.3 per cent in the pre-crisis period. Figure I.1 shows the dramatic changes in the number of bankrupt firms and the unemployment rates in the country before and after the crisis. Changes in unemployment happened mainly in the first four months following the outbreak of the crisis and the rise in bankruptcies. Apart from the rise in bankruptcies of small and medium-sized firms, corporate sector restructuring and legal amendments allowing layoffs were also responsible for the rising unemployment.

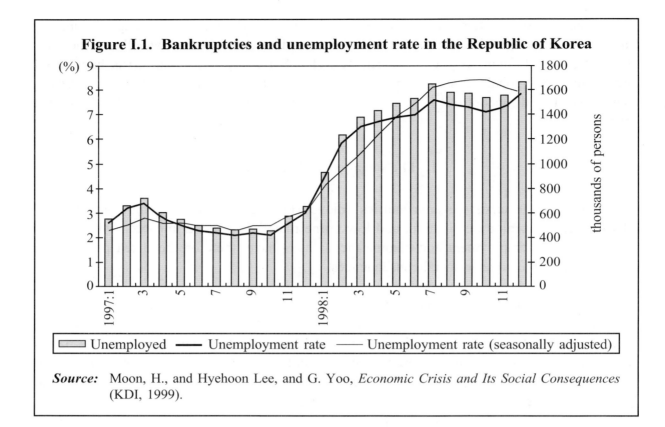

Figure I.1. Bankruptcies and unemployment rate in the Republic of Korea

Source: Moon, H., and Hyehoon Lee, and G. Yoo, *Economic Crisis and Its Social Consequences* (KDI, 1999).

In Thailand, there was a significant rise in unemployment in 1998 after the onset of the crisis. From a 2 per cent low, between 1995 and 1997, unemployment rose to 4.5 per cent in February 1998 with 1.5 million unemployed.

In sectoral terms, the construction sector was hardest hit – its employment reduced more than 30 per cent for both the dry and wet seasons. In the agricultural sector, unemployment was more drastic in the dry season, – 2.25 per cent, than in the wet, – 1.31 per cent. In contrast, the service sector showed a gain in employment during both periods, 5.6 per cent in the dry season and 3.3 per cent in the wet season. This indicates that, in the dry season when the agricultural sector absorbed fewer of the unemployed, they were absorbed in the services and commerce sectors. However, this increase in employment in service and commerce sectors may be due to a shift to the informal sector and, therefore, a sign of an increase in underemployment.

Indonesia went through mild unemployment, the rate increasing from 4.7 per cent in August 1997 to 5.4 per cent in 1998. Such small changes in official figures, however, are cautious statements. The situation in Indonesia is still characterized by an abundant labour surplus. The development and movement of labour, moreover, is not a simple flow from agriculture to non-agriculture or from formal to informal sector and vice versa. It is a triangular flow, from agriculture to informal non-agriculture or to the formal sector, and can move along all directions in the course of an economic contraction (Sigit and Surbakti 1999).

Supporting evidence for this argument can be found in the extremely low wage levels in Indonesia. Even in 1997 the median daily wage as reported by official data was only around 7,500 rupiah in urban and 3,500 rupiah in rural areas, way below the minimum cost of living for a single worker. This indicates that Indonesia did not reach the turning point from labour abundance to labour scarcity. As a result, underemployment is fairly prevalent while the officially unemployed population is very small. It would be groundless then to conclude that the mild increase in unemployment rate of Indonesia implies relatively less severe impacts of the crisis. Unemployment reduced waged income, especially of the low and middle income group who are more vulnerable to the economic crisis. Unemployment also gave rise to pervasive underemployment in the agricultural and informal sectors.

In numbers, Indonesia lost nearly eight million jobs (the equivalent of one in every five modern-sector jobs) in 1998, forcing hundreds of thousands of migrant workers to return home – to more unemployment.

In terms of poverty, by the middle of 1998, the proportion of poor people in Indonesia had reached 24 per cent of the total population of 208 million people – up from 11 per cent in 1996. In Thailand, with its population of about 63 million people, the incidence of poverty increased from 11.4 per cent to 15.3 per cent. And, in the Republic of Korea, the proportion of poor households jumped from around 3 per cent before the outbreak of the crisis to 7.5 per cent, more than double in 1998. Poverty among the country's urban population also more than doubled, from 9 per cent in 1997 to 19 per cent in 1998.

Another impact of the crisis was the rising prices of food and other basic commodities, partly caused by the increasing costs of imports, but compounded in many countries such as Indonesia by the effects of El Niño which had badly affected domestic food production and driven up prices. In addition, some governments had cut price subsidies on basic commodities as they struggled to cope with the financial crisis. For example, Indonesia had cut subsidies on beans, sugar, flour, electricity and fuel. The sudden loss of income, combined with price increases had led to widespread panic and social unrest in the region.

The cut in budgetary expenses as part of the International Monetary Fund (IMF) package of recovery measures adversely affected the education and health budgets of all countries, except in the case of Malaysia where the health budget remained high (Knowles and others 1999). The budget cuts came by way of further reductions in the already under-budgeted items of materials, maintenance and facilities. Regional data indicates that hard-up families were more ready to sacrifice the secondary education of older children than the primary education of younger ones. Moreover the lack of household resources had made for an increase in the utilization of public health services, except in Indonesia where newly increased fees in public health facilities turned prospective users away.

2. Impact on women

Several studies have shown that one of the most affected social groups, whose situation worsened with the onset of the crisis, were women (Moon and others 1999, Park and others 1999, Sigit and Surbakti 1999, Pongsapich and Brimble 1999, and Knowles and others 1999).

In the Republic of Korea, the unemployment rate by sex shows, at first glance, that there was a more severe male unemployment rate as compared to the female unemployment rate (table I.7). While the female unemployment rate increased from 2.3 per cent in 1997 to 5.6 per cent in 1998, the male unemployment shows a drastic rise from 2.8 per cent to 7.6 per cent over the same period.

However, a more careful analysis gives an entirely different view on the status of female labour vis-à-vis the crisis. First, the economically active female population had decreased substantially by 3.7 per cent while the male counterpart increased by 1 per cent. Second, during the same period, the female working age population increased by 1.4 per cent and the economically inactive female population increased by 6.4 per cent.

Table I.7. Changes in labour market by sex, Republic of Korea

(unit: thousands of persons, per cent)

Classification		1997	1998	1999
Male	Working age population (aged 15 or older)	16 887 (1.7)	17 150 (1.6)	17 331 (1.1)
	Economically active population	12 772 (1.1)	12 893 (0.9)	12 889 (−0.0)
	Employed	12 420 (0.6)	11 910 (−4.1)	11 978 (0.6)
	Unemployed	352 (21.0)	983 (179.3)	911 (−7.3)
	Economically inactive population	4 116 (3.5)	4 257 (3.4)	4 441 (4.3)
	Unemployment rate	2.8 (−6.6)	7.6 (171.4)	7.1 (21.7)
Female	Working age population (aged 15 or older)	17 955 (1.6)	18 212 (1.4)	18 434 (1.2)
	Economically active population	8 891 (3.3)	8 562 (−3.7)	8 745 (2.1)
	Employed	8 686 (2.5)	8 084 (−6.9)	8 303 (2.7)
	Unemployed	204 (51.1)	478 (134.3)	442 (−7.5)
	Economically inactive population	9 064 (−0.0)	9 649 (6.5)	9 689 (0.4)
	Unemployment rate	2.3 (43.7)	5.6 (143.5)	5.1 (−8.9)

Source: Moon, H., and Hyehoon Lee, and G. Yoo, *Economic Crisis and Its Social Consequences* (KDI, 1999).

Note: The figures in parentheses represent increased or decreased rates calculated on a year-on-year basis.

It needs to be stressed that female unemployment has a more detrimental impact on female-headed households. This is so because, in general, female-headed households belong to the poorer income groups within the poor population. Evidence of this can be gleaned from table I.8. Looking at the income distribution of livelihood protection beneficiaries by sex of household heads, it shows that over 40 per cent of the female beneficiaries received less than Korean won 100,000 per month, which is almost one-tenth of the poverty line for a four-member household. On the other hand a mere 14.6 per cent of the male beneficiaries belong to this category. The average income of male-headed households is found to be 42.2 per cent higher than female-headed households.

Table I.8. Livelihood protection beneficiaries by income and sex of household head, Republic of Korea

Income Range (Won)	Female Heads		Male Heads		Total	
	Number of Households	Percentage	Number of Households	Percentage	Number of Households	Percentage
<100 000	65	41.4	145	14.6	210	18.2
100 000-150 000	15	10.2	83	8.3	98	8.5
150 001-200 000	13	7.6	129	13	142	35.6
200 001-300 000	21	13.4	247	24.8	268	−23.3
300 001-<400 000	16	10.2	178	17.8	194	40.1
400 001-<500 000	21	13.4	91	9.4	112	8.9
>500 001	6	3.8	123	12.1	129	12
Total	157	100	996	100	1 153	100

Source: *Survey of the Urban Poor in Korea* (Institute of Social Welfare Research, 1995).

In the case of Thailand, the data in table I.9 shows that female layoffs exceeded male layoffs even at the absolute level. Before the outbreak of the crisis, in 1997, female lay-offs recorded 21,748 while male lay-offs were at 23,007. The situation was reversed, however, after the onset of the economic crisis. Female lay-offs reached 29,106, an increase of 36.1 per cent, while male lay-offs decreased from its 1997 figure to 21,748. The proportion of the female workers out of the total number of laid-off workers was 48.3 per cent in the pre-crisis period. The ratio increased to 57.6 per cent in the course of the crisis.

Taking into account the fact that the female labour force in Thailand is smaller than the male labour force, as shown in table I.5, above, the trend clearly indicates that women workers were more affected by the crisis. It is not clear, however whether gender discrimination is the underlying cause of such observed asymmetry across sex. The most massive layoffs took place in the textile industry where 80 to 90 per cent of workers are women. This may be the main reason behind the high layoffs of female workers.

Table I.9. Lay-offs by sex and sector, Thailand, 1997-1998

Type	Number of Establishments		Number of Lay-offs					
			Total		Men		Women	
	1997	1998	1997	1998	1997	1998	1997	1998
1. Garment	16	22	1 590	3 485	617	261	973	3 224
2. Textile	25	18	4 309	8 147	1 025	1 195	3 014	6 952
3. Footwear and leather	14	11	1 423	1 007	431	193	992	814
4. Toys	8	7	600	1 087	86	118	514	969
5. Canned, frozen food	19	50	2 622	1 491	827	664	1 795	820
6. Jewellery	12	9	671	258	327	34	344	224
7. Finance	77	48	5 111	2 005	2 207	843	2 904	1 162
8. Furniture	36	19	2 623	827	2 052	454	571	373
9. Electric and electronic	32	76	3 500	6 080	1 257	1 690	2 243	4 386
10. Spare parts-motorcycles	73	57	3 551	4 881	2 724	3 954	827	927
11. Iron and Steel	25	49	892	2 244	727	1 799	165	445
12. Servicing	90	125	1 678	1 816	905	825	773	991
13. Printing and advertise	16	18	838	803	440	410	398	393
14. Real estate	138	100	4 495	2 765	3 305	2 190	1 190	575
15. Supermarket-mini mart	28	6	1 733	245	524	82	1 209	163
16. Transport	12	44	98	945	80	669	18	275
17. Concrete product	38	34	1 940	2 587	1 350	1 786	590	801
18. Retail trade	95	221	1 178	1 876	618	1 088	560	790
19. Others	149	135	6 173	7 948	3 505	3 126	2 668	4 822
Total	903	1 049	45 025	50 497	23 007	21 381	21 748	29 106

Source: Charoenloet V., *Study on Implementation of Employment/Income Generating Projects to Alleviate Economic Crisis Impacts in Thailand* (ESCAP, 2000).

Table I.10 shows the rather complicated features of the impacts of the crisis on women in Thailand. In the rural areas, for instance, the percentage drop in full time female workers was larger than that of male workers, while in the urban areas there was little difference in the changes between male and female full time workers. As for the urban self-employed, there was an increase of female workers and a decrease for male workers.

The increase in self-employed female workers reflects the active response of laid-off female workers in Thailand. An example of this is a small enterprise called Eden Women Workers, a small garment business network set up by the laid-off women themselves. A survey conducted by the Thai Labour Resource Centre noted that women tend to demonstrate more initiative in job searching and working in the informal sector, while men tend to be easily discouraged when retrenched.

Table I.10. Employed persons over 13 years, Thailand, 1997-1999

(unit: millions of persons)

	Men			*Women*			*Total*		
	1997	*1998*	*1999*	*1997*	*1998*	*1999*	*1997*	*1998*	*1999*
1. Employed persons by hour work									
Rural	12.58	12.00	12.39	10.41	9.97	9.85	22.99	21.97	22.24
Less than 20 hours	0.29	0.41	0.42	0.31	0.39	0.40	0.60	0.80	0.82
20-24 hours	1.00	0.83	1.00	0.98	0.80	0.96	1.98	1.63	1.96
Full time (>24 hours)	11.28	11.26	10.96	9.12	8.77	8.49	20.40	20.03	19.45
Urban	5.45	5.22	5.37	4.57	4.55	4.55	10.02	9.77	9.92
Less than 20 hours	0.05	0.06	0.07	0.06	0.07	0.06	0.11	0.13	0.13
20-24 hours	0.85	0.21	0.25	0.81	0.21	0.23	1.66	0.42	0.48
Full time (>24 hours)	4.55	4.95	5.05	3.70	4.27	4.26	8.25	9.22	9.31
2. Employed persons by sectors									
Rural	12.58	12.50	12.39	10.41	9.97	9.85	22.99	22.47	22.24
Agriculture	8.27	8.58	8.18	7.19	6.77	6.28	15.46	15.35	14.46
Industry	1.15	1.06	1.15	1.06	1.05	1.22	2.21	2.11	2.37
Construction	0.46	0.38	0.31	0.11	0.06	0.06	0.57	0.44	0.37
Service	3.10	2.90	3.15	2.95	3.02	5.59	6.05	5.92	8.74
3. Employed persons by status									
Rural	12.58	12.50	12.39	10.41	9.97	9.85	22.99	22.47	22.24
Employee	3.86	3.53	3.72	2.60	2.50	2.77	6.46	6.03	6.49
Self-employed	5.89	6.18	6.22	2.60	2.14	2.24	8.49	8.32	8.46
Unpaid	2.83	2.79	2.45	5.75	5.33	4.84	8.58	8.12	7.29
Urban	5.45	5.22	5.37	4.57	4.55	4.55	10.02	9.77	9.92
Employee	3.32	3.11	3.17	2.68	2.62	2.62	6.00	5.73	5.79
Self-employed	1.69	1.66	1.74	0.89	0.93	0.97	2.58	2.59	2.71
Unpaid	0.45	0.46	0.46	1.00	1.00	0.96	1.45	1.46	1.42
Total Employment	17.77	17.72	17.76	14.98	14.52	14.40	32.75	32.24	32.16

Source: Charoenloet V., *Study on Implementation of Employment/Income Generating Projects to Alleviate Economic Crisis Impacts in Thailand* (ESCAP 2000).

The situation in Indonesia also shows a mixed picture in terms of the impact of the crisis on employment. Table I.11 shows that the female unemployment rate was higher than the male rates before and after the crisis. With the onset of the crisis, the gender gap shrunk because the male unemployment rate had increased more severely. While female unemployment increased from 5.6 in 1997 to 6.12 per cent in 1998, a growth of 8.51 per cent, male unemployment rose from 4.09 per cent to 5.01 per cent with a growth rate of 22.49 over the same period. Sigit (2000) observed that the crisis affected male workers more severely because the male-dominated sectors were more severely affected, for example, construction.

It is not clear, however, that women workers were less affected by the crisis just because the growth rate of female unemployment was lower than that of the male. It is highly probable that discouragement influences the female labour market as observed in the Republic of Korea. Women who anticipate less opportunity in an adverse labour market may withdraw from job searching activities and join the economically inactive population. In many instances, the movement of workers from the economically active population into inactive population is observed more frequently in the female labour market in a period of economic downturn. This implies that a situation where the labour market is even more unfavourable to female labour in recession. The widespread presumption that women are only secondary income-earners of her household can be partly attributable to such a pattern.

Table I.11 supports the argument that the economic crisis affected women more adversely. The proportion of underemployed women was much higher than men while this order is reversed to over-employment for those working more than 45 hours per week. Since the onset of the crisis, underemployment rose more dramatically among female labour than male labour both in the urban and rural areas. This implies that women had accepted work that paid less rather than remain unemployed. The rise in unemployment among women is lower not because women were affected less by the crisis but because laid-off female labour was more likely to accept lower paid work or swiftly return to the economically inactive population.

Table I.11. Unemployment, underemployment and overemployment by sex, Indonesia, 1997-1998

Location	Less than 35 hours/week				Less than 35 hours/week and looking for work		More than 45 hours/week		More than 45 hours/week and looking for work		Unemploy- ment	
	NSES		NLFS		NLFS		NLFS		NLFS			
	1997	1998	1997	1998	1997	1998	1997	1998	1997	1998	1997	1998
Urban	19.4	21.83	22.01	25.73	2.77	3.62	53.5	49.7	1.43	1.54		
Male	15.26	16.57	16.77	20.11	4.54	6.12	58.5	54.8	2.94	3.18	8.06	9.27
Female	14.81	18.53	31.28	35.46	1.70	2.04	44.6	40.9	0.52	0.50		
Rural	45.99	48.32	48.42	52.38	7.15	7.42	33.5	30.0	1.13	1.34		
Male	37.73	39.69	38.75	42.84	11.38	12.19	42.1	37.6	2.84	3.10	2.84	3.32
Female	59.75	62.70	63.55	66.98	4.86	4.67	19.6	18.2	0.21	0.32		
Total	36.83	39.28	39.45	43.27	5.23	5.67	40.4	36.4	1.26	1.43	4.68	5.44
Male	–	–	–	–	–	–	–	–	–	–	4.09	5.01
Female	–	–	–	–	–	–	–	–	–	–	5.64	6.12

Source: Sigit, H., and S. Surbakti, *Social Impact of the Financial Crisis in Indonesia* (1999).
Notes: NSES stands for National Social Economy Survey and NLFS stands for National Labour Force Survey in Indonesia.

3. Wages and Income

Gender differentials in wages are difficult to compare in the pre- and post- crisis period. In most countries wage data by sex are not collected at the aggregate level. Small sample surveys are an available proxy for wage by sex data, but many of them suffer from lack of representativeness of the sample. As such, this paper refers to some small sample surveys undertaken, with financial support from ESCAP, in the selected countries, Indonesia, the Republic of Korea and Thailand.

Table I.12 summarizes the income changes of 303 beneficiaries of public work programmes in the Republic of Korea. Of the female respondents, 74.2 per cent experienced a 75 per cent drop in income and a 60.1 per cent drop among male respondents. This indicates that women experienced a more drastic fall in income with the onset of the crisis.

Table I.12. Income changes of respondents by sex, Republic of Korea

	No drop	*0-25% drop*	*25-50% drop*	*50-75% drop*	*Over 75% drop*	*Total*
Male	–	–	14 (7.65)	59 (32.2)	110 (60.1)	183 (100.0)
Female	–	–	8 (6.67)	23 (19.2)	89 (74.2)	120 (100.0)
Total	–	–	22	82	199	303

Source: Ohm, Y. S., *A Survey Analysis on the Social Impacts of the Economic Crisis with Special Emphasis on Unemployment Benefits and Small and Medium-sized Enterprises Finance Programs in Korea* (ESCAP, 2000).

From a survey conducted by the Arom Pongpangan Foundation, a labour resource centre in Thailand, it was found that 60 per cent of the unemployed are women aged over 30 years old; 20 per cent had been working in the textile and garment industry. Of this number 213 have been unemployed for a period between 1 to 6 months. Many women have difficulties finding new jobs because of old age, lack of new skills, and low education. A majority of the women, 61 per cent are married and have children. In this regard, Charoenloet (2000) observed that the responsibility of maintaining the family usually falls on the woman when both husband and wife lose their jobs.

The survey by Charoenloet also shows a contrary pattern to that observed in the Republic of Korea. 31 per cent of the female beneficiaries of a microcredit programme belonged to the "no-income drop" group, while only 1.6 per cent of male beneficiaries belonged to this same category. In addition, only 32 per cent of the female beneficiaries experienced an over 50 per cent drop in their income while 44.4 per cent of their male counterparts had the same experience. These findings are consistent with an earlier assertion that, in the case of Thailand, there is insufficient empirical evidence to support the claim that the economic crisis had a more detrimental impact on women.

Table I.13. Income drop of respondents by sex, Thailand

	No drop	*0 -50 % drop*	*Over 50% drop*	*Total*
Male	13 (1.6)	22 (34.9)	28 (44.4)	63
Female	58 (30.7)	71 (37.6)	60 (31.7)	189
Total	71	93	88	252

Source: Charoenloet, V., *Study on Implementation of Employment/Income Generating Projects to Alleviate Economic Crisis Impacts in Thailand* (ESCAP, 2000).

It is observed that, in the Indonesian experience, there is a similar pattern as that found in the Republic of Korea. About 46 per cent of the female beneficiaries experienced more than 50 per cent drop in income drop compared to 35.9 per cent of men in the same category.

Table I.14. Income drop of respondents by sex, Indonesia

	No drop	*Less than 50% drop*	*50% or more drop*	*Total*
Male	57 (22.0)	109 (42.1)	93 (35.9)	259 (100.0)
Lost work	0 (0.0)	5 (14.7)	29 (85.3)	34 (100.0)
Did not lose work	57 (25.3)	104 (46.2)	64 (28.4)	225 (100.0)
Female	12 (23.1)	16 (30.8)	24 (46.2)	52 (100.0)
Lost work	0 (0.0)	0 (0.0)	3 (100.0)	3 (100.0)
Did not lose work	12 (24.5)	16 (32.7)	21 (42.9)	49 (100.0)
Total	69	125	117	311

Source: Sigit, H., *Analysis on Results of Survey on Public Work Projects and Micro-Credit Program in Indonesia* (ESCAP, 2000).

4. Other aspects of the crisis

In general, it has been observed that there was an expansion, across the crisis-hit countries, of women's labour force participation in low-paying work in the services and informal sectors (including prostitution and domestic work) (CAW 1998, 2000; DAWN-APDC 1998). There is agreement, moreover, that women's increased paid work in strongly female dominated sectors was more a result of increased pressure for the family to survive and of the limited opportunities provided by economic systems that carry visible sector-based gender preference. This pattern also indicates the resiliency of certain types of work – mainly those characterized by low pay, casual employment and lack of benefits – during times of economic slowdown.

As if to compensate for the increased dependence of households throughout the region on the incomes earned by women in hard and often dangerous conditions, women have been exhorted to be good mothers and citizens. Women have been asked to sacrifice more for the country and to be more responsible for the well-being of families. Poor women who are already stressed by childcare and earning responsibilities were invoked to be "loyal and supportive of their husbands" (DAWN-APDC 1998).

Social ennui, suicides and crimes were visible throughout the region in the aftermath of the crisis. In the Republic of Korea, 2,300 cases of suicides caused by depression over financial hardships were reported in the first three months of 1998 alone (Kamoltrakul 1999). Official crime rates had increased everywhere (Kowles, and others 1999) and long-standing ethnic tensions erupted into open violence and political instability in Indonesia. Increased abuse of foreign domestic helpers by their employers was noted in a number of crisis-hit countries, the prostitution and trafficking of young women from Cambodia, Lao People's

Democratic Republic, Myanmar and Viet Nam, as well as the exploitation and abuse of unregistered economic migrants from these countries had intensified (Kamolktrakul 1999). The most blatant has been the systematic and growing use of violence against women and young girls as a weapon, including rape in inter-group conflicts.

Women have often been the first workers to be laid off – both because the industries in which they predominate (e.g. garments) are those most affected by the crisis and because women are less unionized and therefore easier to sack. And women – who have primary responsibility for balancing household budgets – have been the ones most directly affected by the changes. Women and girls are also more likely to go short of food than are men and boys.

Other impacts were perhaps less obvious. Research on patterns of expenditure in Asia show that one of the main things on which women had spent their newfound income was on school fees for girls. The widespread cuts in women's income inevitably led to cutbacks in girls' education with obvious adverse implications for the future well being of Asian economies.

C. Policies and programmes to counter the social impact of the crisis

First, a word about social protection and social safety nets. What are social safety nets, and how do they differ from social protection systems? Social protection is understood as the mix of policies and programmes aimed at reducing poverty and vulnerability for individuals unable to work owing to chronic illness, permanent disabilities or old age, and also to protect the majority of the population against some of the unexpected downturns of life (sickness, unemployment, death of breadwinner, etc.). Social security and social safety nets are often used as alternative terms to social protection. Social security generally refers to programmes that are directed at meeting a specific need, that are usually financed on the basis of contributions, and that are available to beneficiaries on the basis of their participation and entitlements. Social safety nets, on the other hand, refer to public measures that are designed to transfer resources to groups deemed eligible due to deprivation. Social protection is intended, therefore, to encompass both social security and social safety nets programmes. In sum, social protection refers to all forms of benefits and services (such as family benefits, universal health care services, and minimum-income provisions) that are generally available on a universal basis without regard to participation, contribution or employment status (although they may include a test of means) (table I.15).

Creating employment and generating income was regarded, from a social aspect, as direct and immediate measures to mitigate the shocks of the crisis. There were many forms of employment and income-generating programmes implemented in the crisis-hit countries. These can be classified into three categories. The first, and most popular, is public works programmes, aimed at helping the unemployed poor, the second, microcredit programmes to assist in financing household expenses and the third is unemployment insurance.

Table I.15. Existing social protection programmes in Indonesia, the Republic of Korea and Thailand, in 1997

Republic of Korea	*Indonesia*	*Thailand*
A. Old age, Disability		
Coverage: Social insurance system covering the employed in firms with 5 or more workers; agricultural workers aged 18-59; voluntary coverage for those employed in firms with less than 5 workers and self-employed. Separate systems for public employees, military and private school teachers.	Coverage: Provident fund system paying lump-sum benefits only, covering firms with 10 or more employees or a payroll above 1 million rupiah per month.	Coverage: Limited social insurance system covering firms with 10 or more employees. From 2 September 1998, voluntary coverage for self-employed will become available. Separate systems for civil servants and private school teachers.
Funding: 6 per cent of payroll paid by employer and 3 per cent of wage earnings paid by employees. Voluntarily insured persons contribute 9 per cent of wage earnings.	Funding: Employers pay 3.7 per cent of payroll, plus 0.3 per cent of payroll for death benefit. Insured persons pay 2 per cent of earnings. Government provides no additional funding.	Funding: Employer pays 1.5 per cent of payroll and insured person pays 1.5 per cent of wages. Government provides annual grant equal to 1.5 per cent of covered wages.
Eligibility: Old-age pension: 60 years of age, insured 20 years or more. Disability: insured at least 1 year, no longer working and disability occurred during the insured period.	Eligibility: Old-age pensions: 55 years of age, 66 months more of contributions. Disability benefit: total incapacity for work and age under 55.	Eligibility: New system. To be payable starting in 1998.
Benefits: Old-age: Non-taxable. Adjusted for price changes. 2.4 times the sum of average of monthly earnings of all insured in the proceeding year and the average monthly earnings of the retiree over the entire contribution period. Total disability: the same as old-age.	Benefits: Old-age, disability and survivor benefits: Lump-sum equal to total employer contributions paid in, plus accrued interest.	Benefits: Disability: same as sickness benefits. A person must have received the sickness benefit for one year. Permanent disability: 50 per cent of prior wage for life.
B. Sickness and Maternity		
The system covers all permanent residents, except government and private school employees and those under Medical Aid program Separate systems for public employees and private school teachers. Funding: employer pays 1-4 per cent (average 1.52 per cent) of standard monthly wage; employees pay also 1-4 per cent (average 1.52 per cent) of standard monthly wage. Government pays a part of the benefits and all administrative costs.	Social insurance system (medical benefits). Coverage being gradually extended to various industries. Employees with more comprehensive benefits exempt from coverage. Employer pays 6 per cent of payroll for married employees and 3 per cent for single employees. Insured persons and government bear no cost.	Limited insurance system with coverage and funding as for old-age pensions. Cash sickness eligibility: 90 days of contribution in 15 months before date of treatment.

(continued)

Table I.15 *(continued)*

Republic of Korea	*Indonesia*	*Thailand*

C. Work Injury

Mandatory public insurance, covering all industrial firms with 5 or more employees. Separate systems for public employees. Employer pays 0.6 per cent to 29 per cent of the payroll, depending on the 'industry risk'. Employees pay no contribution. Government pays the cost of administration. Temporary disability benefits pay 70 per cent of average earnings.
For total disability, annual pension between 138 and 329 days average earnings or lump sum (55 – 1,474 days' earnings) according to degree of disability.

Social insurance system covering firms with 10 or more employees. Voluntary coverage available. Special system for public employees. Employer bears the whole cost, 0.24 to 1.74 per cent of the payroll according to 'industry risk'. Permanent disabilitybenefit varies with the degree of disability with maximum 70 per cent of previous monthly earnings times 60.

Compulsory public insurance covering firms with 10 or more employees, but excluding workers in agriculture, fishing, and a number of other sectors. Funding: employer pays 0.2 – 2 per cent of payroll according to 'industry risk'. Temporary disability: 60 per cent of wages, payable up to 52 weeks.

D. Unemployment Insurance

Coverage and eligibility: In January 1998, it will cover firms with at least 10 workers. To qualify, employees must be employed for at least 12 months during 18 months before involuntary unemployment occurred. Benefit, financed by 0.6 per cent payroll tax shared between workers and employers, is equal to ½ of the average worker's daily salary during the preceding 12 months.

No programmes

No programmes

E. Social Assistance

Korea's social assistance system consists of two components:
(i) public assistance (livelihood protection, medical aid, veteran relief, disaster relief): and
(ii) social welfare services (for the disabled, elderly, children, women and the mentally handicapped). Public assistance provides services and financial assistance to needy people with low incomes. Social welfare services focused on maintaining family welfare of the disadvantaged groups.

No programmes

No programmes

Source: United States Department of Health, Education, and Welfare, *Social Security Programs throughout the World 1997* (August 1997 and Gupta and others, 1998).

1. Indonesia

The public works programmes in Indonesia, adopted to mitigate the shocks of the crisis, are a revival of programmes that go back to 1994. These earlier programmes were designed to provide employment opportunities to workers in infrastructure construction. With the onset of the crisis, these programmes were revised to accommodate the needs of laid-off skilled workers. Therefore, the public works programmes had two components: one aimed at alleviating the impact of drought (Proyek Dampak Kekeringan Dan Malsalah Ketenaga Kerjaan, PDKMK) and the other aimed at reducing lay-offs of skilled workers (Proyek Penanggulangan Pengangguran Tenaga Kerja Terdidik, PTTT).

PDKMK is a large national project implemented in all 27 provinces of Indonesia. The public works programmes include road-hardening, construction/repair of village roads, normalization of irrigation and rivers, construction of public markets and small shops, planting of useful plants in unused government land, and construction of fishponds and nets for culturing seawater fish. The important criteria for selection of the activities are that the outputs of the works must be useful and can be followed up.

PTTT was introduced to assist the laid-off skilled workers by providing credit and training to encourage them to become own-account workers. Strictly speaking, however, PTTT is not a public works programme.

Microcredit programmes in Indonesia are called KUKESRA, an acronym referring to credit for family welfare. The main objective of these programmes is to empower families by providing soft credit at low interest rates through a simple and quick procedure for the development of their economic activities. The credit is given to individuals, but they are required to organize themselves in groups. The groups consists of families at different levels of welfare mutually interacting to enhance their productive economic activities.

As a complement to microcredit, the Government provided credit to small- and medium-sized firms that were home-based or focused on household development activities. There are many constraints in developing economic activities for microcredit recipients, most of whom live below the poverty line. These include the lack of access to technology and marketing skills. Linking microcredit recipients with other more capable economic agents would improve their weaknesses. Credit for small- and medium-sized firms provides incentives for firms to cooperate with the targeted families.

2. Republic of Korea

Soon after the onset of the crisis, the Republic of Korea adopted a variety of policy measures including public works programmes, microcredit programmes, and expansion of unemployment insurance to counter the detrimental impacts of the economic crisis.

Unemployment insurance refers to the various benefits to enhance the employability of workers such as educational and training services, subsidies for childcare, and job placement services. This programme was first introduced in 1995 and, with the crisis, underwent a series of expansions. Initially, the programme covered firms with more than 30 regular employees.

Within a year after the outbreak of the crisis, it was expanded to cover all firms. From October 1998, employees of all firms including those with less than 5 workers, including regular, part-time, and temporary workers, became eligible for unemployment insurance.

Eligibility for the programme include: i) a minimum contribution period of 6 months, ii) involuntary termination of employment status, and iii) active job searching after layoff. The period of duration for benefits ranges from three to eight months depending on the age and contribution period. For example, a worker under the age of 30 and with a contribution period between six months to a year will receive a minimum wage as unemployment benefits for three months.

The average benefit level is half the average wage prior to the termination of employment. However, there is an upper and lower limit for the benefit. Highly-paid workers are limited by an upper ceiling of 30,000 won per day, while poorly-paid workers, half of whose wage is below 90 per cent of minimum wage, will be paid 90 per cent of the minimum wage during the pre-unemployment period.

As indicated by the title of the programme, enrolees are required to pay their contribution for at least six months. Once an enrolee fulfils this minimum contribution period and is involuntarily laid-off, he/she is eligible for benefits equivalent to 90 per cent of his/her average monthly wage for six months. For those who are still unemployed, even after the termination of the benefit, a special extension of two months will be given.

Despite the immediate expansion of the unemployment insurance scheme, financial assistance to most of the unemployed was not provided due to the minimum contribution period requirement of 6 months.

For those who are not eligible for unemployment insurance benefits, the government introduced public works programmes. Public works programmes can be an effective means of providing temporary income support to the unemployed without distorting their work incentives. Workers are paid for their productive work and not merely subsidized with living costs. Local governments provided temporary jobs for the unemployed in their regions, which include street cleaning, traffic control, parking guides, forest conservation, etc. Public works suitable for women such as computerization, information projects, and assistance at social welfare facilities were later added.

The benefit period was initially set at three months and later extended to six months in July 1998. The payments ranged from 22,000 won to 35,000 won per day. Taking into account the fact that the poverty line for a four-member household was 793,476 won at that time, the benefit level is considered to be adequate income protection. However, the benefits were even higher than the minimum wage leading to work disincentives, which runs counter to the purpose of this scheme, which is to provide for productive welfare.

3. Thailand

The Government of Thailand placed high priority on employment creation given that the unemployment rate jumped from 1.5 per cent in 1997 to 4.4 per cent in 1998. The first step was to launch the Miyazawa package, a public works programme financed by the World Bank, Japan Exim Bank, and OECF. The Miyazawa package was an expansionary fiscal policy aimed at boosting the shrunken economy and helping the poor affected by the crisis.

Under this programme, external borrowings are distributed from the central to the provincial/district levels. Each district is equipped with 100,000 baht to be spent on job creation ranging from reservoir digging, drainage clearing and earth-filled road construction. The District Administrative Council is responsible for overseeing the work performed by the beneficiaries and its outcomes.

The Government designated a portion of the World Bank loan for a microcredit programme to promote social investment. For this purpose, two funds were set up – the "Social Investment Fund (SIF)" and "Regional Urban Development Fund (RUDF)". The former programme targets local and community grassroots organizations to induce them to implement development projects, with a fund of US$120 million. The latter programme is a revolving fund loaned to municipalities for their capital investment projects. The budgets allocated to these two funds are managed by the Social Fund Office (SOFO), a non-governmental organization, under an innovative method known as the 'bottom-up' system. SOFO selected projects are implemented by communities and budgets are granted to them.

The SIF aims at projects initiated by local community organizations, municipalities, and other informal groups such as cooperatives, women's groups, environmental protection groups, or groups associated with religious organizations or schools. Projects under the SIF are required to be representing the theme of promoting the foundation of a civil society all over the country and good governance at different levels.

Eligibility for investment under the SIF requires that projects fall under specific categories. The first set of categories is community economy projects. These include community demonstrations and learning centres, community markets, training in production and marketing of products, and community water supply. The second set includes community welfare and safety finances, community child development and day care centres, community playgrounds and shelters for the elderly and HIV/AIDS patients. The third set is characterized by natural resource management and cultural preservation themes. These include activities around mangrove preservation, forestry management, and cultural preservation. The fourth set encompasses community capacity building and networking activities. Finally, the fifth set covers emergency community welfare financing and immediate community welfare assistance needs arising from the economic crisis. A newly added component in the fifth category allows for social assistance transfers through community organizations for vulnerable groups most severely affected by the economic crisis.

D. Evaluating the programmes from a gender perspective

There have been several studies on the causes, magnitude, and consequences of the Asian crisis. However, little has been done to evaluate the effectiveness of the programmes implemented to counter the detrimental impacts of the crisis. All the crisis-hit countries have launched various policy measures to assist the most affected groups, at least in purpose, and at great expenses. It is essential, therefore, that these programmes be evaluated as a first step toward improved policy measures to enable the countries to achieve more effective social protection schemes.

As previous research has shown, women constitute one of the most vulnerable groups and were adversely affected by the crisis. Most of the policies and programmes, however, were designed and implemented without accommodating gender perspectives. Implementing programmes without particular attention to women may lead to a worsening of gender inequality and prevent women from receiving adequate and timely benefits.

Experience has shown that, a more thorough understanding of the magnitude of the detrimental impacts levied on women and the effectiveness of the policy responses aimed at alleviating such burdens, can lead to devising policies and programmes that are not only gender responsive but socially sustainable.

One factor contributing to the lack of progress in the impact assessment of social safety net policies is the lack of availability of relevant data. For this reason, ESCAP had conducted and financed small sample surveys to evaluate the effectiveness of selected programmes in three countries – Indonesia, the Republic of Korea and Thailand. The main purpose of these surveys is not to grade and compare overall performance, but rather to draw valuable implications from the experiences of these three countries in their design and implementation of policies. In this context, ESCAP selected four types of social safety net schemes: public works programmes, microcredit programmes, credit to small- and medium-sized firms, and unemployment insurance for the surveys. In the following sections, an overview of these findings will be presented, with a fuller analysis appearing in the subsequent country chapters.

1. Public works programmes

Public works programmes (PWP) were implemented in all the three aforementioned countries. The evaluation survey, however, covered the PWP schemes in Indonesia and Thailand only.

The PWPs in Indonesia were found to be unsuccessful in protecting women against the sudden loss of employment and income as a result of the crisis. First, the proportion of female labour among the PWP beneficiaries was very low despite an unusually high proportion of female unemployment and underemployment in Indonesia.

One of the main reasons for the extremely low representation of female beneficiaries may lie in the selection of jobs offered by the PWP. It was observed that the jobs selected were more suitable for men than women, for example construction, repair, renovations and normalization of infrastructure, etc. These works generally require physical strength to a great extent. Even though the PWP expanded the scope of the works to include agricultural labour such as planting of unused land, in-land fishery, animal husbandry, construction of water sewage systems and village streets, production of cement bricks, construction of small shops in local markets, and normalization of tertiary irrigation channels in the later stage, these are still more designed for male labour.

Another observation from the survey is that the majority of the respondents perceived the selection process to be a fair one (table I.16). 98.3 per cent of respondents affirmed the fairness of the selection process. This indicates that the majority of women do not recognize unfairness in the selection process. Only three out of 292 respondents expressed negative perceptions regarding gender fairness in the PWP.

One explanation for this may lie in the fact that there were no explicit requirements excluding women from the PWP benefits. In fact, there were no particular requirements for participation and the broad guidelines were that the beneficiaries should be economically disadvantaged, a group which includes youth, women, the unemployed, those displaced from work, school drop-outs, or the poor.

In reality, however, there was an excess demand for the PWP and therefore applicants were subject to an informal screening process based on a priority list formulated at the local level. Social leaders and village officials decided who would be the beneficiaries. There is no statistical evidence supporting sexual discrimination in the selection process at the district level. Nevertheless, the widespread presumption that women are secondary income-earners of households may have influenced local-level decision-making on participant selection.

Additionally, information on the existence and application procedure of the PWP was provided to the potential beneficiaries mainly through the Government and social leaders. Over 90 per cent of the potential beneficiaries were informed by the Government and social leaders. Table I.17 shows that no one obtained the relevant information on the PWP through the news media, and hence, it was relatively easy to exclude particular groups from receiving the information. Government officials and social leaders at the local level are likely to be influenced by the traditional prejudice that women are secondary income earners and, therefore, priority be given to men, who are perceived as the primary income earners.

More importantly, the low representation of female poor in the PWP resulted from a gender-biased task selection process. Many do not recognize the gender bias incorporated in the task selection process as a serious problem. But it is. If there is an evidently gender bias in task selection, then the PWP inherently prevents women from participating, even if there was a gender-balanced selection procedure for recipients. It appears, however, that there was a gender bias both in the type of work and the participant selection process in the Indonesian case.

Table I.16. Evaluation of the selection process of PWPs in Indonesia

Selection Fairness		Selection Procedure Fair	Type of Discrimination				
			Gender	Races	Religion	Politics	Total
No	Simple	12	1	1	0	1	15
	Complex	2	0	1	0	0	3
	Total	14	1	2	0	1	18
Yes	Simple	270	0	0	0	1	271
	Complex	17	3	0	1	0	21
	Total	287	3	0	1	1	292

Source: Sigit, H., *Analysis on Results of Survey on Public Work Projects and Micro-Credit Program in Indonesia* (ESCAP, 2000).

Table I.17. Sources of information on PWPs in Indonesia

Information Sources	Benefited		Did not benefit		Total Number
	Number	Percentage	Number	Percentage	
Government	233	74.9	78	25.1	311
Family/Friend	47	15.1	264	84.9	311
Employment Agent	1	0.3	310	99.7	311
News Media	0	0.0	311	100.0	311
Social Leaders	110	35.4	201	64.6	311
Others	0	0.0	311	100.0	311

Source: Sigit, H., *Analysis on Results of Survey on Public Work Projects and Micro-Credit Program in Indonesia* (ESCAP, 2000).

The PWP in Thailand shows a somewhat different picture from the Indonesian case. Females dominate males in the proportion of beneficiaries. It is unclear, however, if this gender distribution is the result of policy design or the fact of the more active participation of women in the Thai situation. As discussed earlier, a large proportion of Thai women who, after being laid-off, immediately started small businesses of their own or formed themselves into small networks of garment manufacturers. As observed by the Labour Resource Centre of Thailand, women took more initiative in job searching activities and moved into the informal sector while men tended to be easily discouraged. If there is a tendency for women to more actively search for work, then the high proportion of female participants in the PWP may not be an outcome of progressive gender consideration in design, administration, and actual enforcement of the programmes.

A statement in an official document is evidence that the main target group of the PWP is male labour between 40 and 60 years of age. The actual participants, however, turned out to be young males in their twenties and thirties, and women mainly retrenched from textile factories. One plausible explanation is that the PWP was unsuccessful in "capturing the workers" most affected by the crisis. The economic crisis began in 1997, but focus group discussions revealed that the massive influx of workers laid off and returning to the countryside only began in 1999. It is possible, therefore, that the PWP adopted at the early stage of the crisis did not protect those most affected by the crisis.

The experiences in Indonesian and Thailand show a number of contrasting perspectives of women's status within a social protection programme. One common element, however, is that in both cases the main target group of the PWP was male labour.

2. Microcredit programmes

The microcredit programme (MCP) in Indonesia was designed to assist in family planning. As such, the main target group was women. The MCP was initiated by the Family Planning Coordination Board, and was originally an extension of the family planning programme. One motto in the family planning campaign was "small family means better welfare". The incentive to sustain the achievements in birth control and to attract more participants was that families joining the programme experience a substantial increase in their welfare.

Accordingly, microcredit was given to eligible women participating in the birth control programme in order to help them start small businesses or enlarge their on-going business. The main rationale behind this programme was that better living standards would weaken the incentives to rely on their children as a present source of income and/or for old-age security.

Eligibility for this programme was extended only to women from low-income households. This programme later developed into a more general one, not tied with the implementation of family planning programmes. Nevertheless, the eligibility criteria in the initial stage were maintained on the whole.

As table I.18 shows, there was an unusually high proportion of female beneficiaries in the MCP – 95.4 per cent of all respondents were women. This situation appears to be inconsistent with the observations made earlier regarding the PWP where male respondents expressed a more severe decline in their income compared to women respondents. 40 per cent of male interviewees reported an income reduction of more than 50 per cent; in contrast 25 per cent of females reported similar income reductions. More explicitly, 34.8 per cent of females did not experience any drop in their income while 17.6 per cent of males reported the same experience.

This situation may be explained by fact that the MCP in Indonesia is female-oriented and that only the relatively more adversely affected males participated in this female-oriented programme. It is perhaps a reverse situation in the PWP, which was more suitable for men and which saw the participation of women who were more seriously affected.

Table I.18. Demographic and economic classification of MCP beneficiaries, Indonesia

Gender	Income Drop			
	No drop	*Less than 50%*	*50% or more*	*Total*
Male	3 (17.6)	6 (35.4)	8 (40.1)	17 (100.0)
Lost work	0	0	0	0
Did not lose work	3 (17.6)	6 (35.4)	8 (40.1)	17 (100.0)
Female	102 (34.8)	118 (40.3)	73 (24.9)	293 (100.0)
Lost work	5 (45.4)	4 (36.4)	2 (18.2)	11 (100.0)
Did not lose work	97 (34.4)	114 (40.4)	71 (25.2)	282 (100.0)
Total	105	124	81	310

Source: Sigit, H., *Analysis on Results of Survey on Public Work Projects and Micro-Credit Program in Indonesia* (ESCAP, 2000).

Table I.19 summarizes the overall performance of the programme as an employment or income-generating scheme. The proportion of working participants shows a slight rise and the growth rate is about the same across sex. It may be observed also that, although the purpose of the credit was to generate income-generating activities among housewives, it seems that the credit was used to provide work opportunities for all household members.

Table I.19. Average number of working respondents, Indonesia

Income Drop	Before Participation		After Participation	
	Female	Male	Female	Male
No drop	108	109	114	117
Less than 50 %	86	107	94	111
More than 50 %	105	75	114	91
Total	98	99	106	108

Source: Sigit, H., *Analysis on Results of Survey on Public Work Projects and Micro-Credit Program in Indonesia* (ESCAP, 2000).

Although the microcredit programme was initially designed to target women, it appears that they did experience some discrimination in the process. Table I.20 presents the major complaints on the MCP. The highest frequency of complaints reported referred to discrimination. A majority of the respondents, 52 per cent out of 310 respondents, affirmed that MCP is affected by discrimination. The reason for this situation may lie in the highly complicated bureaucratic procedures and insufficient funds allocated by the MCP. The fact that 32 per cent of total respondents complained of insufficient credit may be supporting evidence to this argument.

Table I.20. Complaints on microcredit programme, Indonesia

	No Problem	Small Amount	High Interest Rate	Not Able to Repay	Discrimi-nation	Others	Total
No Income Drop	0	27	0	4	69	5	105
Less than 50 %	1	45	0	14	52	12	124
50% or More	0	27	1	6	40	7	81
Total	1 (0.3)	99 (31.9)	1 (0.3)	24 (7.7)	161 (51.9)	24 (7.7)	310 (100.0)

Source: Sigit, H., *Analysis on Results of Survey on Public Work Projects and Micro-Credit Program in Indonesia* (ESCAP, 2000).

The microcredit programme in Thailand was mainly offered to those who operate small businesses, to assist them to sustain the business or invest in capital formation in order to expand their employment capacity. The latter was the case with the unemployed workers' cooperative. The majority of beneficiaries were women (189 out of 252 respondents).

One may interpret such a high proportion of female beneficiaries as favouring women. However, cultural particularities should be taken into account in understanding this high female representation. When the crisis hit Thailand's economy, women, particularly laid-off women in their forties, were the most affected population group. Expected to earn incomes to feed their families but unemployed, some of their spouses left them for other women

(Charoenloet 2000). In Thailand, women are no longer supplementary income earners; rather, they are the main or the primary income earner in some cases. This may explain why the majority of beneficiaries of the MCP are female.

There were, however, observations of gender bias against women in the administration process and the requirement criteria for the MCP in Thailand. For example, the MCP requires a well-written application form and a proposal with a clear objective of the project. But, the illiteracy ratio among women is double that of males. Moreover, the lower education level of women may prevent needy women from being selected as beneficiaries. Given the great discrepancy in illiteracy across gender and the lower educational level of women, requiring a well-written proposal can create critical gender bias.

One thing to note in the MCP in Thailand is that the required documentation gives rise to and strengthens close relationships between NGOs and the affected population groups. This is to ensure the probability of being selected. The MCP was implemented through two channels: individuals or groups. Group applications were encouraged because the most important aim of MCP was to promote the development and cooperation of community and civil society. In reality, it was not an easy task to organize business groups for several reasons including lack of leadership and management skills, and excess demand for funds. The easiest way for an individual to be a member of a group application was to form a close relationship with NGOs. Traditionally, female representation in community-based NGOs has been low. Policy-level emphasis on group applicants and low female participation has possibly contributed to another type of latent gender bias against women in the microcredit programme of Thailand.

3. Unemployment insurance

The Republic of Korea is the only country with unemployment insurance among those affected by the crisis. Unemployment insurance is operated on the basis of the voluntary contributions of enrolees. Due to difficulties in administration, small businesses with less than five workers, in general, do not provide unemployment insurance benefits.

Possible gender bias against women in unemployment insurance can arise in a number of ways. First, from the population coverage; the proportion of female labour is relatively high in small businesses, and generally not included in the unemployment insurance scheme. Second, from the required entitlement condition that beneficiaries be actively seeking jobs. Thirdly, gender bias may arise from the eligibility requirement that beneficiaries are involuntarily laid off.

It has been observed that, despite the expanded eligibility conditions to all workers, there is still a large proportion of small businesses with less than five workers and firms not enrolled in the unemployment insurance scheme. Given that female labour experienced a high frequency of lay-offs in the course of the crisis, such a low proportion of female beneficiaries implies under-representation of women in unemployment insurance.

Eligibility conditions for unemployment benefits require that beneficiaries are unemployed and actively searching for new job opportunities. As discussed earlier, however, female workers were severely discouraged by unfavourable labour market practices during the drastic economic downturn, thereby giving up their search for new jobs. They became part of the economically inactive population who are classified as non-unemployed. The low official unemployment rate of female labour and the unusually drastic increase in females among the economically inactive population implies that even the majority of women discharged from the formal sector did not meet the entitlement condition.

Another requirement for eligibility is the involuntary termination of employment. In most cases, firms forced the laid-off candidates to retire voluntarily, at least in the formal documentation. Moreover, from the employees' perspective, many felt ashamed to be laid off involuntarily and requested that they be classified as voluntary retirees. Therefore women, the first population group laid off in the course of the corporate and financial sector restructuring process, were induced to apply for voluntary retirement. As such, they were not eligible for unemployment benefits. Many who followed the instructions and guidance of the firms did not even recognize the existence or detailed eligibility conditions of unemployment insurance.

Another main pillar of income security in cases of job loss is the retirement allowance, under which anyone who terminates employment receives an average monthly wage multiplied by the number of working periods at the workplace. Any employee who is hired by the firm with more than five workers is eligible for the allowance regardless of voluntary or involuntary termination. This allowance provides better protection than the unemployment insurance benefit in most cases because unemployment insurance provides 50 per cent of an employee's previous salary for a maximum of six months. On average, workers employed by the same firm for more than three months will receive higher benefits from the retirement allowance.

Even though the responsibility of payment of retirement allowances was imposed on all work places with more than five workers through legal compulsion, most of the firms did not put aside sufficient funds for payment of the allowances. In the wake of the crisis, and following massive bankruptcies of firms, many job losers were not protected by this allowance scheme. To help them, the Government established a special fund that pays retirement allowances and unpaid wages of the bankrupt firms.

However, a large proportion of female workers are excluded from the retirement allowances because they were working in informal and small businesses, which are not covered by the Labour Standard Act. In line with this, female labour in the Republic of Korea did not sufficiently benefit from either the expansion of the unemployment insurance scheme or from the establishment of the Wage Guarantee Fund.

E. Conclusions

Where formal social protection systems do not have sufficient human and financial resources to cover identified needs, the priority will be to target available resources to vulnerable groups. Progressively, comprehensive social protection systems will be developed but, in the short term, resources will be channelled to those most in need. Matching the results of social expenditure reviews and vulnerability analysis will show the need to either pursue the development of a formal social protection system or concentrate scarce resources into priority needs and short-term social safety nets. When the vulnerability analysis shows high child/adult dependency ratios and children exposed to risks, the country's social protection system should target children. When most vulnerable people live in the rural areas, resources should be decentralized and programmes be put in place to target these priority population groups. A distribution analysis should ensure any proposed social protection programme achieves its targeted objectives.

Special consideration should be paid to gender issues. Although half of the population of all population are women, they receive much less assistance and opportunities than do men. Many poverty reduction and social development programmes are focused on households and do not consider intrahousehold differences. Assets and labour are normally distributed in a different and unequal manner between men and women, boys and girls within a same household. Unless particular attention is paid to women's unique problems and life patterns when social protection policies and programmes are developed, approaches that might appear to be gender-neutral may actually disadvantage women. Positive discrimination may be needed to ensure women's development in this region. For example, labour market reforms must go beyond a purely traditional agenda to adequately address such special concerns of women as a higher incidence of home work, competing demands from household responsibilities, and the particular needs surrounding child bearing. In child protection, the benefits of investing in the girl child are large – educated girls become more responsible and better-informed mothers. Social insurance programmes need to be designed to take into account the longer life expectancies of women in most societies; the additional implications for women of the risk of loss of support due to death, abandonment, or divorce; and the less stable earning patterns commonly found among women.

The most vulnerable populations are often not reflected in household surveys – migrant workers, orphans, the homeless, victims of disasters, refugees, nomads and marginalized indigenous groups. These groups may require special attention owing to both extreme poverty and social exclusion. As with women, they may be seriously disadvantaged by programmes that appear otherwise to be uniform and fair, owing to the effects of labour market discrimination and alternative cultural traditions. Special outreach strategies are normally required for those.

CHAPTER II.

INDONESIA

In the two decades prior to the 1997/1998 crisis, Indonesia's growth rates averaged between 6 and 8 per cent. The Government had invested heavily in basic health care and education to improve the quality of the labour force. Labour-intensive manufacturing for export led the way to higher incomes and dramatic reductions in poverty. 64 per cent of all Indonesians were poor by international standards in 1975; fewer than 11 per cent in 1995.

But when capital began to flee the country in 1997, financial panic turned quickly into bankruptcy and massive unemployment. Currency devaluation pushed import prices skyward, soaring inflation squeezed all nonessential items out of family budgets. Indonesia's economy shrank by 5 per cent in 1998, the number of poor more than doubled.

As in other crisis-hit countries, no social or economic group was untouched by the press of rising prices, falling wages, widespread unemployment, and the expanding wave of business failures. However, women workers bore a disproportionate share of the labour market adjustments triggered by the crisis. The crisis doubled unemployment rates between 1997 and 1998, and although women made up just over one-third of the labour force, they made up more than 46 per cent of Indonesia's unemployed. Although fewer women than men were affected by unemployment, women's income dropped much further than men's suggesting that enterprises were replacing male workers by lower-paid women. The increasing unemployment and poverty also resulted in many women turning to the commercial sex industry in order to find work and support their families. Report after report during the crisis years expressed details of how women were being affected, not only in terms of unemployment but in the areas of reproductive health care and education as well.

As with most of the other crisis-hit countries in the region, Indonesia did not have in place an adequate social protection system to mitigate the shocks of the crisis on its vulnerable citizens. What few schemes that existed covered only workers with formal sector employment. This excluded from coverage most agricultural employment, occasional or part-time employment, domestic service, and informal sector employment – sectors in which Indonesian women workers predominate. Information from Indonesia suggests that, in the initial stages of the crisis, the poor relied primarily on their relatives, neighbours, and other community members as a safety net to cope with their unexpected misfortunes (Indonesia, Consultations With the Poor 2002). For example, several communities in Java reported a form of rice-aid known as *Perelek or Jimpitan*. Participating households contribute one cup of rice every month, and this pot is then used to give rice loans to needy families. When rice is given to old or people with disabilities, no repayment of the loan was required. Institutions like the *Perelek* or *Jimpitan* are evidence of community solidarity, and they show the resourcefulness of the poor, especially in the absence of adequate formal social protection.

Within a year of the crisis, however, the Government did set up a number of social safety net schemes, and reformed some existing ones. This chapter examines social protection schemes that existed in Indonesia prior to the 1997/1998 crisis, the social safety net initiatives put in place during the crisis, and future plans for an improved social protection system for the country. The chapter will also examine if the social protection schemes reflect the different circumstances of women and men in the labour force.

A. Social impacts of the crisis

What available statistics there are show that the contraction in Gross Domestic Product (GDP) which occurred in 1998, in Indonesia, was most severe in the non-agricultural sectors of the economy, especially in construction, the financial sector, wholesale and retail trade, non-oil manufacturing and transport. All these sectors registered contractions of more than five per cent. It has also been in these sectors, especially construction and financial services that employment fell most rapidly. Indeed the labour force surveys conducted since 1997 indicate that there has been no net growth in non-agricultural employment between 1997 and 2000.

The population living below the poverty line increased significantly from 22 million (11 per cent of total population) in 1996 to 49.5 million (24 per cent) in 1998. The swelling in the ranks of the poor was even more dramatic because Indonesia was hit by the confluence of the financial, political and El Niño shocks.

The total number of unemployment was estimated at 13.7 million in 1998, the rate having risen from 4.9 per cent in August 1997 (before the crisis hit) to more than 15 per cent in December 1998 (ILO 1998). The contraction in non-agricultural output and employment, together with the surge in inflation in the middle of 1998, had an especially serious effect on the poor, because food prices rose more rapidly than non-food prices. Hence, poor households consumed food of lower quality (and quantity); their children faced the risk of dropping out from school; and they could not afford basic health services. A variety of reports indicate that millions of children had not returned for the 1998 school year. School enrolment and drop out rates were mixed: in rural areas more girls were dropping out of school than boys, while the reverse was true in urban areas (World Bank 1999).

It has to be remembered, however, that the household surveys carried out to estimate the impact of the crisis on poverty, income distribution, and unemployment did not consider that part of the population who do not live in registered households. To the extent that numbers of unregistered street dwellers have increased in urban and peri-urban areas since 1997, and to the extent that many of them have expenditures below the official poverty line, they are excluded from the poverty estimates

As far as most wage and salary workers were concerned, the effects of the rupiah devaluation and the ensuing inflation were almost wholly negative. Real wages in all sectors of the economy fell steeply in late 1997 and 1998, and appear to have made only a partial recovery since then. Urban dwellers suffered a greater decline in income especially in the initial phase of the crisis, but the rapid inflation of 1998 led to a surge in the cost of living for farmers. Given the large increase in the agricultural labour force that occurred between 1997 and 2000, it is unlikely that there will be a strong upward pressure on agricultural wages for some time to come.

In addition, the price hike also impacted the quality of public services. Many local health centres and hospitals could not retain their services due to the high price of drugs and medical equipment. In the education sector, primary and secondary schools and universities could not operate at the same level as before the crisis.

As costs increased for basic household goods, women must make difficult decisions on how to allocate diminishing household funds. Health care workers in Indonesia reported that more pregnant women were cutting costs by turning to traditional healers or family members to attend their labour (New York Times 1998). Oxfam International reported that on the Indonesian island of Flores, visits to health care centres had declined dramatically because families could not afford to pay for services and even basic antibiotics were unaffordable (Oxfam 1998). Childhood immunizations had been nearly universal in Indonesia, but with the onset of the crisis, vaccinations for measles, mumps, and rubella became too costly for poor families (Washington Post 1998).

Much of the adjustment to the fall in labour demand came through a decline in real wages. Unemployment and underemployment increased significantly in Indonesia, where women, in particular those aged 25 and older, scrambled to supplement household resources in the wake of huge income drops (Horton and Mazumdar 1999). There was considerable informalization of work, as labour shifted out of the formal sector and out of employee status into self-employment, unpaid family work and agriculture. The relatively larger (smallholder) agriculture sector appears to have acted as a shock absorber, leading to smaller increases in open unemployment in the country.

The Indonesian experience has been captured in a series of longitudinal studies conducted by the RAND Corporation at the request of the Government of Indonesia and a consortium of donor organizations, including the United States Agency for International Development. Between August and December 1993, researchers first interviewed members of 7,200 Indonesian families to determine family experiences and perceptions concerning employment, education, health care, and community involvement. In follow-up surveys conducted in late 1997, just before the crisis hit the archipelago, 94 per cent of the original families were interviewed.

In mid-1998, one-fourth of the same families were again interviewed to ascertain the effect the crisis had on household behaviour. This survey's findings do not provide conclusions representative of the general population but do offer keen insights into the dynamics of family adjustments to the crisis. According to RAND researchers, before the crisis, just over 49 per cent of Indonesian women were working. By August 1998, this number had increased to more than 56 per cent. But this increase was entirely the result of women working as unpaid labour in family-run enterprises. The fraction of women surveyed working at paid employment increased by a statistically insignificant 1 per cent, from 36 per cent to 37 per cent.

Before the crisis, Indonesians had been migrating from rural settlements and remote islands to the country's major cities. The crisis reversed this tide as jobless workers returned to their villages and farms. A labour surplus accumulated in the countryside, the first consequence of which was a spiralling decline in real wage rates. Soon, those with jobs had to work longer hours to make ends meet. Men worked more hours per week at paid employment than did women (34.7 hours for men, 31.6 hours for women), but women increased their work effort by 2.7 hours a week, more than the increase for male workers.

In terms of international migration for work, there were five women migrants for every male migrant from this country in 1998 and 1999, compared to three men for every two women in 1983-1984.

Labour markets can make a variety of adjustments to a decline in demand for paid labour: workers can be laid off, hours can be cut back, or wages can fall. Indonesian workers found themselves straddling an ever widening chasm of shrinking incomes and rising prices.

Regional droughts had already cut deeply into crop production, especially rice, pushing food prices ever higher. The crisis forced cutbacks in Government subsidies for milk and rice, while exchange rate depreciation increased the price of imported food. Together, these factors accelerated inflation in food prices. In addition, employers "bid down" the wages of paid labour. Real wages fell between 20 and 30 per cent in 1998. The declines were largest for men in the urban sector, smallest for rural women. Overall, RAND concluded "apparently, the lion's share of the labour market adjustment to the crisis has not been in terms of hours and employment but in terms of real wages".

Taking family location and size into account, RAND found that families with young women (ages 15 to 24) were less likely to sink into poverty and more likely to rise out of poverty than were other families. These women entered the labour market to help maintain family incomes, often replacing older women who were laid off. The fraction of younger women working at paid employment increased significantly over the year; however, the fraction of women as a group remained statistically unchanged.

Another report (UNFPA 1999) found that one of the responses to increasing unemployment and poverty is that many women were turning to the commercial sex industry in order to find work and support their families. A Jakarta based foundation reported that the number of women and girls entering prostitution had increased fivefold between 1997 and 1998 (World Bank 1999). Moreover, women who lost jobs in factories and who turned to commercial sex reported that their earnings as sex workers were lower than they had been as factory workers, because their clients could not afford to pay them appropriately. Overall, the report found that the economic crisis had an immediate adverse impact on the lives of individuals, especially women and girls, in the areas of reproductive health care, education and employment.

B. Social protection and social safety nets

1. Pre-crisis schemes

As in many other parts of the Asian region, Indonesian policy makers have in the past voiced their reluctance to have "western-style" social security provision which is supposed to destroy entrepreneurial initiative and lead to a culture of welfare dependency. The Asian model of development rested on the assumption that export-led employment of a well-educated, flexible labour force could eliminate poverty and ensure employment security. This laissez-faire approach may have been responsible for the most dramatic reduction in poverty in history, but it also left these countries particularly vulnerable.

The most important income security protections in Indonesia, prior to the crisis, are employer-provided provident funds. Firms with 10 or more employees (or firms with payrolls greater than a mandated ceiling) are required to contribute 3.7 per cent of their payroll to provident funds for employees, who also contribute 2 per cent of their earnings. The accounts provide lump sum benefits for pensioners over 55 with five and a half years of contributions or to younger workers who are completely disabled.

The social security benefits for civil servants and armed forces include payment for retirement savings and pension, and health care. For private sector employees covered in the social security scheme for private-sector workers, the benefits include employment injury, insurance, death compensation and retirement insurance. A compulsory health insurance scheme for civil servants, which was established in 1968, was reformed in 1991 to provide comprehensive medical care to registered members and their dependants under the managed health care system.

A savings and insurance scheme was also set up in 1977 for civil servants. It provided endowment insurance and pension benefits. Civil servant employees are required to contribute to the scheme and a lump sum payment is made to the contributors upon their retirement, or in the event of death. The monthly pension scheme also requires monthly contributions, which is a fixed percentage of monthly wages.

A social security scheme for private sector employees was first established in 1978 and replaced with a new one in 1992. Private and state enterprises with 10 workers or more were able to participate in this scheme. The benefits of the scheme were fourfold: compensation for work-related accidents, death benefits, old age benefits and health care.

Apart from the aforementioned schemes, the Government of Indonesia had, prior to the crisis, set up public works programmes to generate employment and income during difficult economic times. These earlier programmes were designed to provide employment opportunities to workers mainly in infrastructure construction. The programmes were administered by the Department of Manpower and applied to socially useful projects with the intensive use of labour inputs, and with wages not exceeding the market rates for unskilled labour. In 1994, however, the Government discontinued these programmes.

All the aforementioned programmes, however, were never intended to relieve the widespread hardships inflicted by an economic crisis.

2. Post-crisis schemes

In an effort to address the social impact of the crisis, the Indonesian Government implemented several social safety net (SSN) programmes beginning in 1998. The main objectives of SSN programmes are to:

- provide ample security for the provision of basic food at affordable prices to the poor;

- provide health services to the poor and education services for the children of the poor;

- create productive employment to increase purchasing power of the poor;

- generate community-level economic activities.

As the adverse impacts of the crisis became more and more apparent, and worsened by the prolonged drought, the Government decided to revive its earlier public works programme at the end of 1997. BAPPENAS (National Development Planning Agency) assumed the planning functions for the renewed scheme and district/municipal governments were given primary responsibility for the selection of areas and project, identification of beneficiaries, and budget expenditure. The PK-1 or "crash programme", as it came to be referred to, was focused on Java and especially in the 10 principal urban areas surrounding Jakarta, Surabaya, and Bandung, as well as other districts/municipals affected by the ongoing drought.

In 1998, the Government decided to expand the public works programme into a national social safety net to cover the whole country. 33 billion rupiah was allocated to this programme of emergency, labour-intensive infrastructure improvements employing the equivalent of 54,000 workers for 80 days. For 1998 and 1999, the Government allocated 600 billion rupiah for rural and urban infrastructure development and another 500 billion rupiah for labour-intensive forestry, creating roughly 103 million workdays of employment.

Other programmes were also implemented. A total budget of 9.4 trillion rupiah was allocated to fund 15 programmes as follows:

- Food security: special market operations for rice (OPK) and national food security programme through farmers empowerment (PKPN-MPMP);

- Social protection in education: scholarships and school block grant, scholarships and university block grants, operations and maintenance of school facilities, primary school rehabilitation, and specific block grants for primary school construction;

- Social protection in health: social safety net on health sector (JPS-BK), social welfare (JPS-BS), and supplementary food for primary school students (PMT-AS);

- Productive employment generation: labour intensive programme in public works sector (PKSPU-CK), labour intensive programme to eradicate crisis impacts (PDKMK), labour intensive projects for skilled work forces (P3T), labour intensive programme in forestry sector, and empowerment of the regions to overcome the impact of the economic crisis (PDM-DKE).

Food security programmes

The Special Market Operation for Rice (OPK) programme provides poor households with 20 kgs of rice per month at subsidized prices (1,000 rupiah/kg). The programme was targeted to reach 14.6 million poor households in all provinces. In addition to the regular OPK programme, which is operated mostly by Government officials, the Government also cooperated with several NGOs to deliver rice. This was part of the World Food Programme assistance to needy families.

Another food security programme, the OECF-funded Development of Poultry Rural Rearing Multiplication Centre (RRMC) was aimed at increasing food stocks (meat and egg) in rural areas and generating new employment by increasing poultry production and productivity.

The Rehabilitation of Brackish Water Shrimp Culture Infrastructure programme was directed to poor farmers. In this programme, infrastructure for shrimp culture was developed and agro-inputs provided to poor farmers. The budget of the programme was 54.1 billion rupiah (an OECF loan), and implemented in 10 provinces.

Social protection: education

One of the educational programmes is the Scholarships and School Block Grant scheme. The programme is targeted at 1.8 million primary school students, 1.65 million junior high school students, and 0.5 million senior high school students who hail from poor families.

Social protection: health

In the area of health, the Social Safety Net on Health Sector (JPS-BK) programme is a multi-year programme funded by the Asian Development Bank (ADB). The programme provides a "health card" to poor households, which can be used to receive free health services from local health centres and hospitals. This multi-year programme is funded by ADB and implemented in 13 big cities.

The Supplementary Food for Primary School Students (PMT-AS) is a nationwide interdepartmental programme. In addition, the students' parents may also receive incremental income by preparing food using local sources.

Employment and income generation

The objective of the Labour Intensive City-Wide Urban Infrastructures and Services Programme (PKP) is to absorb unskilled and poor unemployed persons in urban areas through the implementation of construction/rehabilitation or operations/maintenance of urban infra-structures.

The low participation of women in previous labour-intensive programmes justified the implementation of this demand-based programme. Theoretically, any organization in urban areas may submit a proposal on proposed activities such as social services, operations and maintenance of infrastructures, and training, with the objective of absorbing female unemployment.

Community empowerment funds

The Empowerment of the Regions to Overcome the Impact of the Economic Crisis (PDM-DKE) programme was aimed at increasing the purchasing power of the poor by generating employment through labour-intensive activities and/or providing revolving funds for small-scale businesses. The most important aspect of the programme is that community groups have to plan the programme themselves with the assistance of facilitators in designing, implementing and monitoring the activities proposed.

The target groups of this programme are urban and rural poor who are unemployed and unable to afford sufficient food, health, and education services. Rp 792 billion was allocated to fund the PDM-DKE programmes in all provinces.

It should be noted that, the latest three programmes, PKP, SIWU, and PDM-DKE, were not implemented in the fiscal year 1999/2000 due to budget limitations. Political uncertainties and several pending, high-profile corruption cases had delayed the disbursement of several loans aimed at supporting the budget deficit.

Safeguarding activities

Beginning in the fiscal year 1999/2000, several safeguarding activities were carried out to maximize the effectiveness and efficiency of the programme, especially in reaching the intended beneficiaries. These included the improvement of the quality and coverage of information dissemination, establishment of complaint resolution mechanisms, application of performance-based reporting system, independent verification, and the enhancement of civil society participation. In order to ensure the implementation of these safeguarding activities, except in the case of independent verification, the Government established the SSN programmes Management Coordinating Team at the central, province, and district/municipal levels. These teams consist of two units, the SSN Information Centre (SSN-IC) and the SSN Complaints Resolution Unit (SSN-CRU).

Transparency and information dissemination

The SSN Information Centre (SSN-IC) was established with the objective of actively disseminating information on SSN programmes, and to ensure that any interested party has access to SSN data and information. In addition to these customer-based services, the SSN-IC at district/ municipal level also produced the "SSN Information Folder" which contains brief information on the SSN programmes and their detailed budget allocations in each administration. At the national level, the SSN Information Clearinghouse also disseminates information through several publications, bulletins, the internet and national newspapers, television and radio stations.

In addition, each programme-implementing agency also disseminated information through several modes, such as television and radio stations, newspaper, and local government officials at sub-district and village level.

Civil society participation

Learning from the first year experiences of the SSN, the Government supported the establishment of "stakeholders' forums" (FLP) in every district/municipality and at the national level. In the operational stage, all civil society stakeholders and the Government are enabled to discuss complaints, issues, and problems in the public sphere.

Citizens' participation is not only limited to the FLP. Most SSN programmes involve civil society representatives in the targeting process at local level. Recent observation shows that this involvement is effectively increasing the quality of targeting. In addition, several nationwide NGOs were also being consulted in the process of programme guidelines preparation and served as independent evaluators for several programmes.

Performance-indicators-based reporting and independent verification

Reporting is a standard procedure in the implementation of any programmes/projects. To assess the performance of SSN programmes, the reporting system is designed to measure performance based on agreed indicators and against the agreed targets for a particular indicator. Based on reports from each implementing agency, the Coordinating Team issues the SSN Monthly Performance Report that is verified by an independent team. The controlling team, which consists of government officials and NGO representatives, was established to verify these reports and to control the overall implementation of SSN programmes.

Grievance mechanism

A complaint resolution unit (CRU) is established not only within the SSN Coordinating Team, but also embedded into each programme- implementing agency. The unit's main task is receiving and taking necessary actions to follow-up each complaint within a certain period. Another important characteristic of the CRU is that it should report to the complainant and the general public (through FLP) of the corrective actions that have been taken.

Other poverty reduction initiatives

In addition to social safety net programmes implemented by the Government, there are several Government-executed programmes and also a number of private initiatives with poverty reduction objectives.

Kecamatan development programme (KDP)

A pioneering effort in the cultivation of new social safety net initiatives is the *kecamatan* development programme (KDP). The programme is aimed at addressing the needs of rural communities in combating poverty. It has developed approaches for providing support to both private sector economic activities as well as public infrastructure development. It was among the first efforts to directly finance activities of local communities and incorporate the participation of the poor themselves. It was initiated before the crisis and re-designed to mitigate the negative impacts of the crisis in rural areas.

Urban poverty programme (UPP)

To reach the urban poor in Java, an urban counterpart to the KDP was put in place. The project's objective is to empower local communities to overcome poverty in urban areas. The project provides a revolving fund to the community for sustainable income generation by groups and individuals within their jurisdictions. The programme also aims to finance the development of community-selected basic infrastructure and employment generation activities in low-income urban areas. The project initially targeted the poor in some 60 local Government jurisdictions in the northern half of Java, especially in Yogyakarta, Malang, and Bandung where most of the country's dense urban areas and small industries are located. The total population of these targeted areas is about 24 million. Other areas were to be targeted in the following phases of the programme. The project will provide financing for sustainable economic activities demanded by the community groups themselves. Funds for the support of private economic activities will have to be repaid within two years with interest rates at commercial levels. One half of the interest repayments will be made available and used to help finance the maintenance of local public infrastructure. Funding for small public infrastructure in local communities will be on a grant basis. Workers engaged in these activities will be paid the local minimum wage.

Village infrastructure programme (VIP – P3DT)

This programme, aimed at improving and providing infrastructure for poor villages, had been in place long before the crisis and continues to this day. The programme has proved successful in assisting the rural poor strengthen their economic as well as social activities. Rural roads, drinking water, sanitation, and other infrastructures considered necessary by the poor are included in the programme activities.

Community recovery programme (CRP)

The CRP is an innovative civil society-led mechanism aimed at strengthening the coping capacities of vulnerable segments of the population especially those most severely affected by the crisis. The objective is to channel resources to support local community-based organizations in the implementation of assistance activities. Programmes funded under the CRP primarily focus on enabling and empowering local communities and beneficiaries to help themselves. The objective of CRP is to establish an effective non-governmental mechanism, which can respond to the needs of the poor in a rapid transparent and inclusive manner. The CRP will work across a variety of substantive areas: food security, basic and social services, and employment and income generation. The CRP reports to a Civil Society Consortium, which is comprised of both Government and non-government members. The project has established a trust fund into which donors can make contributions.

C. A gender evaluation of the crisis-initiated social safety nets

As a programme that was planned and implemented within a very short time period, PK-1 experienced many problems in its execution. One of the major setbacks was "targeting"; many of the beneficiaries were not selected correctly (inclusion error). For example, because of the high wages provided by this programme many students and those already actively employed were selected to join the programme. Moreover, the activities selected were not productive and as such did not provide any other benefits (externalities) except cash transfers. Importantly, women were disproportionately represented in these programmes.

In its first year of implementation, the SSN programmes experienced numerous problems that led to many complaints and criticisms. The Government also conducted internal evaluations on the performance of SSN programmes, with the assistance of academicians and other parties. There were also civil society networks conducting independent reviews. Significant in this process were the recommendations that emerged from a Government-civil society consultation held in April 1999 to discuss the monitoring and evaluation of the SSN programmes.

Based on the experiences of the first year programmes, and somewhat improved socio-economic conditions, the budget allocation for the SSN programmes, for fiscal year 1999/ 2000 was reduced to 5.6 trillion rupiah aimed at 12 programmes. Improvements in Year 2 programmes included the use of more accurate and up-to-date data in the targeting process, establishing programme implementation monitoring (safeguarding) activities, programme integration, and emphasising women's participation. Moreover, the allocation of funds to the lower levels of implementation was done at district/municipal level – and in certain instances, even at smaller administrative units – allowed flexibility by accommodating the unregistered poor, and involved more non-governmental parties.

Learning from the first-year experiences, many stakeholder meetings were convened and 13 recommendations were agreed upon to improve SSN programmes for the fiscal year 1999/2000. Based on the aforementioned recommendations, several improvements were incorporated into SSN programmes in the second year. These included: (1) an improved database for more accurate geographic targeting, (2) promoting a gender responsive programme, and (3) improved coordination between the programme and stakeholders through establishment of the National Coordinating Committee of SSN programmes. The coordinating Committee is mandated to improve the safeguarding of the programme through five activities, i.e. (1) transparency and information dissemination, (2) a complaint resolution system, (3) a performance reporting system, (4) independent verification of performance reports, and (5) involvement of as many stakeholders as possible in every step of programme development and implementation.

Of all the SSN programmes of 1998, the Employment Generation Programme was the most criticized for the lack of or absence of participation by women. The activities selected, mainly maintenance of public infrastructures such as road, irrigation and urban sanitary system, made it difficult, if not impossible for women to participate almost right from the start.

The Programme of Empowering Regional Capacity to Alleviate Impacts of Economic Crisis or Pemberdayaan Daerah dalam Mengatasi Dampak Krisis Ekonomi – PDMDKE, however, has seen a significant participation by women. In this programme, the community decides on the programmes according to their situation. As such, some communities have chosen rural employment generation or microcredit schemes, or social services provision. Women's participation in these programmes varied according to regions. In Aceh and West Sumatra, women's participation exceeded that of men's. In West Java, women's participation was more than 31.8 per cent, and in many other areas women participation's was more than 28.3 per cent.

Many SSN programmes have provided women with increased opportunities to participate in health support services. Special interventions were made for pregnant women, lactating mother and mothers with young children.

In the Educational Support programmes, poor girl students were the main targets of the programme. This was aimed at keeping them in school, given the tendency for female students in poor families to be taken out of school when the household is financially insecure.

Additional measures were taken to ensure an improved participation and representation of women in the second generation of SSN programmes. In fact, equitable opportunity for women and men as SSN beneficiaries has been made one of the performance indicators of a successful programme. For employment generation, a completely revised programme was initiated in urban areas, in which women's participation is an important performance indicator for the programme. The revised programme had two subprogrammes, i.e. Urban Employment Generation Programme, and the Special Initiative for Unemployed Women. Both programmes were designed to be demand-driven; employment is provided on demand, and the participation of women is targeted.

The Programme of Special Initiative for Women Unemployed (SIWU) was launched in response to the many criticisms that women were excluded from the employment generation programmes despite the fact that they were severely affected by the crisis. In this programme, employment generation took a 'bottom-up' approach in implementation. Proposals were made by local community organizations and the selection of participants decided by a multi-stakeholder local committee. Activities allowed for in this programme ranged from social services to infrastructure maintenance, and each proposal was expected to absorb around 70,000 unemployed poor.

In Indonesia, the SSN programmes were initiated with the aim to help protect the traditionally poor and the newly poor. In other words, the intended beneficiaries of these programmes are the needy which may not be able to cope with impacts of the crisis without outside assistance. This implies that the effectiveness of these programmes can be measured by their coverage of the poor and what benefits of the programmes have reached the poor. However, given the geographical coverage and the need to speed up implementation, there were difficulties and problems encountered in planning, implementing, and monitoring these SSN schemes. The issue of mistargeted and misused funds were reported in the media and these shortcomings were also acknowledged by the Government. BAPPENAS, for example, admitted that about 8.6 trillion rupiah out of the total 17.9 trillion rupiah of SSN funds in the fiscal year 1998/1999, was misbudgeted, and used to fund "supplementary" programmes. However, as discovered by the Independent Monitoring Task Force, in some cases these were not strictly SSN programmes.

Further, anecdotal evidence indicates that, unfortunately, in many cases the programmes had largely missed the target groups, chief among them being women who were severely affected by the crisis. Nevertheless, it should be emphasized that the effectiveness of the programmes varied across programmes and regions. Some programmes had both high coverage amongst the poor and showed reasonable and effective targeting, while some programmes in some districts performed poorly.

A study done by SMERU (1999) in West Java found that, in general, access to SSN programmes tended to decline noticeably with distance from the local centre of policy and decision-making. The further a hamlet is from the village office, the less likely it is to be involved in the SSN programmes. At the same time, the SSN programmes were not distributed evenly throughout the region in the spatial sense. A disproportionately large number of scholarship beneficiaries was recorded in hamlets in one district, while most of the village credit was concentrated in two or three hamlets. In some areas, respondents had never even heard of the Padat Karya programme, while in others no one was aware of the existence of the Special Rice Programme.

Overall, several reports pointed to only two successful programmes, the Back to School Programme and the OPK rice subsidy. As argued by Jacquand (1999) the scholarship programme was perhaps the most impressive of the SSN programmes because of its efficient targeting and the tangible assistance that it provided. The OPK was also successful although several weaknesses were found in its implementation. Based on an evaluation by SMERU in five provinces in Java, several improvements are crucial for the improvement of OPK including extending public information and improving locally based targeting.

Apart from misbudgeted funds, a portion of the funding was also not channelled to the most needy groups of the population; in other words it was mistargeted. A study conducted by the Ministry of Finance to evaluate the implementation of the SSN schemes in Java estimated that of the core SSN schemes, around 411.746 billion rupiah was lost to corruption and 518.096 billion rupiah was lost to mistargeting.

By definition, SSN programmes are aimed at helping the most vulnerable segments of society to help them deal with serious short-term social needs. In fact, as shown in the Indonesian case, it is difficult to determine what is included and what is excluded under SSN programmes. In other words, the entire design of the SSN programmes in Indonesia suffers from a lack of clarity and transparency regarding target groups and forms of assistance.

Moreover, there was considerable confusion as to what could be classified as truly SSN schemes. Particularly in the first year of its implementation, there were activities categorized by the Government as SSN schemes that had neither the characteristics nor the functions of SSN schemes. Further analysis on the plethora of the SSN activities in Indonesia showed them to be composed of the following: (1) newly designed initiatives such as CRP; (2) old programmes that have been revised such as the Padat Karya; (3) reoriented existing programmes that were implemented primarily through sectoral programmes; and (4) expansion of existing poverty alleviation programmes.

While the SSN schemes initiated by the Government were wide ranging, there is a general perception that these schemes are fragmented. These schemes neither seemed to contain a coherent policy framework nor financing-targets and monitoring systems. Interventions were targeted at specific sectors with almost no cross-sectoral influences factored into the design. Programme design was almost totally divorced from macro-planning processes, and therefore lacked an integrated approach in the overall national recovery efforts.

In addition, it is very important to include gender aspects into the SSN programmes. As women and girls have shared the impacts of the crisis but they have not always shared the benefits of the response programme, it is very crucial to take gender into consideration in developing SSN programmes. For example, women make up only a small fraction of the construction and forestry workforce; the public works programmes did not offer much relief to women workers.

In brief, the main task is to move beyond a situation of immediate relief, streamline the policies and define an effective long-term approach. In other words, there is an urgent need for the Government to establish a much broader and longer social welfare policy. Two reasons lie behind the urgent attention to the design of a comprehensive policy of social welfare, of which the SSN is but one element. First, social expenditure constitutes the largest component of the Government budget. Second, a prolonged economic crisis, accompanied by a rise in poverty, implies that social assistance will remain at the forefront of the policy agenda in the coming years.

The agenda for the future: From a crisis response to a sustainable system of poverty reduction and social protection for all

The fiscal year 2000 was set to be the last year for the implementation of SSN programmes. Thereafter, the focus was to be on sustainable poverty alleviation programmes. Some of the SSN programmes are already incorporating features of sustainability. The health programme, for instance, is developing an insurance scheme that will provide participants with affordable and accessible health care on a long-term basis. More importantly, the Government has planned for extensive discussion among all stakeholders regarding future crisis efforts. The major task that lies ahead is the reorientation and/or scaling back of SSN initiatives with a view to evolve programmes tailored to address structural poverty and sustainable economic growth.

Several poverty reduction programmes, focusing on community empowerment, are already being developed. The Kecamatan (sub-district) Development Programme and Urban Poverty Alleviation Programme are but two examples. These programmes, designed to involve partnerships with the private sector and the community themselves, are the shape of future mainstream poverty reduction policies to come.

Decentralization and the future of local stakeholders' forum

In line with the newly legislated law on local autonomy that allows district/ municipal governments more authority to design and implement their own development programmes, local governments will play an important role in arranging specific needs-based poverty reduction schemes. Importantly, there is a need to build the capacity of local governments to be more responsive to the development needs of their region.

It is also important to strengthen the local stakeholders' forum to reflect the "customer service revolution" that makes consumers become co-producers in decision-making processes. Such forums are important for at least two reasons. First, civil society has access to updated information on development programmes and can respond immediately when problems occur. Second, there is a need to enhance the sense of ownership and responsibility in the designing, implementing and monitoring of programmes.

A well-run district/municipal level stakeholders' forum should not limit their concerns merely to SSN schemes, but other poverty reduction and development programmes as well. In the future, the forum may incrementally increase their authority and responsibility; for example in designing local poverty reduction strategies and programmes, in the targeting process, in the verification of the programme implementation progress and in complaint resolution reports, or even being transformed to be a complaint resolution unit itself.

Enhancement of safeguarding activities

The activities to safeguard SSN programmes are part of efforts towards good governance. These efforts, however, should not be limited to "pilot programmes". There is a need to develop a civil society mechanism to ensure accountability in Government programmes.

Improving the quality of safeguarding activities is a never-ending process. Quality control and adequate information dissemination should be enhanced to avoid asymmetrical information among programme stakeholders. This will help eliminate moral hazards such as corruption. Verification of progress reports produced by the Government will also ensure that the agencies implementing the programmes provide realistic data, take necessary corrective action in the short term and improve programme design in the long run. In terms of grievance mechanisms there is a need for communities and civil society groups to feel confident that all complaints will be followed up by necessary corrective actions. One way to achieve this is to ensure the involvement of relevant institutions such as the police, district attorneys, and the Government's internal auditor in the grievance mechanism.

Pro-poor and gender specific approaches.

Information and data on the poor, their numbers and location, status in the community, etc. needs to be collected and monitored carefully and systematically. Sex-disaggregated data is also extremely important. In this regard, the capacity of local governments and community groups should be enhanced. Several recommendations for future poverty alleviation programmes include the following:

- First, every development effort should provide easy and affordable access for the poor to participate as beneficiaries of development. Special attention should be given to projects that will provide adequately for the poor, men and women, with jobs and income opportunities.

- Second, further actions for the poor should be developed in health and education services programmes. Young children, pregnant and lactating mothers are a strategic target group for future programmes in these areas.

- Third, programmes linked to food security are strategic actions to be developed in the future, as contingencies in times of crisis. Agricultural development, food processing and storage systems, and information on food availability and accessibility must be enhanced and managed on a needs-based system.

- Fourth, in areas with a high incidence of poverty, special programmes should be developed and managed in a sustainable fashion. Programmes such as PDMDKE, linked to community empowerment initiatives remain relevant to the poor.

- Fifth, community capabilities and social systems that support the poor should be encouraged, for example, zakat and fitrah practised in Muslim societies, which are important systems to finance poverty alleviation efforts.

D. Conclusions

Social safety nets are short-term responses to mitigate the negative impacts of the economic crisis on the poor. SSN safeguarding activities, however, are an essential part of good governance. In line with the democratisation and decentralization processes currently underway in Indonesia, good governance practices and the involvement of civil society in decision-making processes reflect the future shape of development in Indonesia.

An integrated policy on poverty eradication is necessary to ensure that Indonesia's development is "pro-poor". The previous approach to development, emphasizing economic growth, may have been responsible for the most dramatic reduction in poverty in history, but it also left the country particularly vulnerable in times of crises such as the recent one. Economic and social policy must be integrated. This implies, first, social sector development such as education and health, should receive more attention and become an integrated part of the poverty reduction policy. Second, there must be fair allocation of resources. In agricultural-based economies such as Indonesia, equitable land distribution is crucial. There must also exist a mechanism to enable the poor access to resources. Third, efforts must be stepped up to improve the capacity of local governments and community groups in poverty alleviation programmes. Fourth, poverty reduction programmes initiated by the Government, and those implemented by the private sector and civil society should be integrated.

It has often been argued that there is an inherent conflict between the direct promotion of short-term social safety net activities and the long-term sustainable economic growth. Not focusing on immediate, near-term efforts on the poor, however, will in fact impede long-term economic development. Poverty alleviation and social safety net efforts can be geared to augmenting viable long-term human and physical capital assets and thus the stimulation of growth.

CHAPTER III.

REPUBLIC OF KOREA

The Republic of Korea has been a star performer in terms of economic growth, industrialization and poverty reduction over the past three decades. In a little more than one generation the country moved from an underdeveloped agrarian economy to an industrialized society. Experiencing a booming economy for over thirty years, the country paid little attention to the social protection for the unemployed. In the late 1980s, technological and industrial changes led to a reduction in job opportunities. Subsequently, the Government enacted legislation to intervene in the labour market for assisting employment adjustment. More legislation was introduced up to the mid-1990s to provide retraining schemes and employment services for disadvantaged workers With the 1997/98 crisis the Government went even further in expanding the social protection system to provide better employment services and social security systems, although traditionally the state was reluctant to intervene in the social functions of the family.

The 1997/98 crisis was especially harsh on women. When the economy hit the skids, tens of thousands of female workers were sacked. Even in the restructuring process of 2000, women were still first on the firing line. Although unemployment fell from a record of nearly 10 per cent in 1998 to less than 5 per cent in 2000, the situation for women in the workforce did not improve. More women were forced to sign part-time contracts as companies cut operating costs. Women are also became redundant in record numbers at banks – historically one of the nation's biggest employers of females – as branches tossed out tellers and replaced them with electronic cash machines. Women flocked to advertising and marketing jobs, where they were able to carve out a niche for themselves, but openings soon became scarce. Women's civic groups were reporting that more women in their late 20s and early 30s were turning to prostitution. In 2000, the authorities conceded that the number of wonjo-kyoje, or younger women dating older men for pocket money, was "increasing rapidly" (Businessweek Online, July 24, 2000).

The Government of the Republic of Korea has carried out, in the last decade, several significant legal and policy reforms to improve women's status in the country. In 2000, the Ministry of Gender Equality was established to develop and implement various national policies to advance the status of women and to achieve gender equal society. There are also specific social protection policies designed for disadvantaged women.

This chapter examines the situation of women, especially in terms of the impact of the crisis, their employment status; and assesses the adequacy of social protection schemes, and crisis-initiated social safety nets, in meeting the needs of women in the country.

A. Social impacts of the crisis

The most important channel through which the crisis had an impact on the majority of households was through a reduction in the demand for labour. The Republic of Korea experienced the sharpest increase in open unemployment as compared to the other crisis-hit countries: the unemployment rate went up from 2.5 per cent just before the crisis, to a peak of 8.7 per cent in February 1999, before declining to 4.6 per cent in October 1999 (World Bank, 2000a). In addition, a large number of people gave up searching for new jobs upon becoming unemployed and thus became part of the economically inactive population. Between the second quarter of 1997 and the fourth quarter of 1998, the economically inactive population had increased by 9 per cent or 1.2 million people. Most of the newly unemployed were low-paid workers – the temporary and daily workers, the self-employed and unpaid family workers – and therefore would not have benefited from unemployment insurance. The deterioration in the Gini coefficient for real per capita income is a reflection of the particularly adverse impact of the employment shock amongst these more vulnerable workers.

1. Rising unemployment

The crisis put many of the modest gains made by women in the past several decades at risk. Problems faced by women were twofold: first, they were squeezed out of the labour market and, second, they experienced a worsening in their working conditions. Women tended to be the first to be laid off, and their security of employment deteriorated severely. In 1994, about 38 per cent of working women were in regular employment, while 62 per cent were in casual or temporary positions. By 1999 this had dropped to only 30 per cent in regular jobs and 70 per cent in casual or temporary positions.

Women suffered disproportionately in the economic crisis for a number of reasons. They were, in general, to be found in lower paying positions and had considerably less seniority than men. Women were also predominantly irregular workers, a situation that worsened after the crisis. Additionally, small and medium sized companies bore the brunt of bankruptcies and closures following the crisis, and these firms were the mainstay of women's employment. 62.5 per cent of women workers were employed in companies with less than five employees at the time of the crisis (Rhie 2000).

Table III.1. Unemployment rate in the Republic of Korea, 1997-1999

(unit: 1000 persons, per cent)

By quarter		Number of unemployed people (unemployment rate)	Males (unemployment rate)	Females (unemployment rate)
1997	3/4	470 (2.1)	300 (2.3)	170 (1.9)
	4/4	560 (2.6)	358 (2.8)	202 (2.3)
1998	1/4	1 179 (5.6)	790 (6.2)	389 (4.7)
	2/4	1 481 (6.8)	1 004 (7.7)	477 (5.5)
	3/4	1 597 (7.4)	1 083 (8.3)	514 (5.9)
	4/4	1 587 (7.4)	1 055 (8.2)	532 (6.2)
1999	1/4	1 748 (8.4)	1 170 (9.3)	578 (7.0)
	2/4	1 435 (6.6)	973 (7.5)	462 (5.2)
	3/4	1 220 (5.6)	823 (6.3)	397 (4.4)
	4/4	1 010 (4.6)	679 (5.2)	331 (3.7)

Source: National Statistical Office, (NS0, 1990-1999) Annual Report on the Economically Active Population Survey, each year.

2. Employment

Although unemployment rates were higher among male workers than females since the economic crisis, female workers' employment levels declined more rapidly than male workers, and hence the Asian crisis actually inflicted greater damage on female workers' employment levels. Between 1997 and 1998, for instance, male employment declined by 510,000 (-4.1 per cent), but female employment dropped by 602,000 (–6.9 per cent). Consequently, women's share of total employment declined by one percentage point.

One study confirms similar results (Kim 2000), and argues that the reduction in demand for labour due to the economic crisis affected female workers more adversely than male workers. The seemingly contradictory phenomena arose, because, on the one hand, new male entrants to the labour force experienced greater difficulty in getting jobs than their female counterparts, and on the other hand female workers lost jobs more rapidly than male workers. Moreover, once female workers were retrenched, they were more inclined to withdraw from the labour market as compared to male workers, as shown in the sharper increase in the economically inactive population among females than males. The same study confirms that job-seeking rates were lower among the female unemployed than among the male unemployed since female unemployed workers were more likely to withdraw from the labour force. The study further confirms that since the eruption of the economic crisis, employment rates among the unemployed declined among both male and female workers and reached more or less the same level (around 22 per cent) in 1998, but the re-employment rate was higher among female workers before the crisis. Female re-employment rates declined more rapidly than that of male workers.

Interestingly, female employment fell relatively more in those industries and occupations where female workers are more represented than in other places, and male workers' share in those same industries and occupations increased since the economic crisis. This is indicative of some degree of substitution of male workers for female workers during the economic crisis.

While employment of male workers increased in electricity, transportation, storage, and finance industries, as well as business, private and public services and other industries, the number of female workers in these industries decreased, indicating some degree of substitution of female workers by male workers. By occupation, while male workers increased in administration, service, and sales occupations, female workers employed in these occupations declined sharply, again implying that there was a certain degree of substitution between male and female workers.

Going by employment status, male workers maintained their status before and after the crisis. However, among female workers, the proportion of regular (permanent) workers declined, while daily female workers' share rose substantially, suggesting that some of the former regular or temporary female workers might have shifted their employment status to daily workers.

Ahn (2000) confirmed similar findings in a dynamic context. In the case of males who lost regular jobs, 38 per cent found regular jobs. By contrast, only 31 per cent of laid-off female workers landed regular jobs. While 22 per cent of the males who lost regular jobs found non-regular jobs, 26 per cent of the females landed non-regular jobs. This non-regularization of female workers was reinforced by the trend among those who lost non-regular jobs. Only 6 per cent of the unemployed workers who lost non-regular jobs found regular jobs subsequently, and as many as 59 per cent of them obtained non-regular jobs. For males, these rates were 8 per cent and 53 per cent and for females, they were 5 per cent and 63 per cent respectively, demonstrating that female non-regular job holders found it more difficult to transform themselves to regular job holders. These findings indicate that, since the economic crisis, female workers must have increasingly occupied a greater portion of non-regular jobs unless this trend was offset by an opposing trend among new entrants to the labour force.

Nationwide statistics on the total wage earners report that the proportion of daily female workers had steadily increased from 16 per cent in December 1997 to 21 per cent in December 1998 and to 25 per cent in November 1999. Based on these figures, it can be concluded that female workers' employment status had, since the onset of the crisis, steadily deteriorated toward non-regular jobs characterized by lower wages.

3. Involuntary unemployed

Another study tries to analyse gender differences in unemployment, especially in the causes of unemployment, using unemployment insurance statistics (Cho 1999). In the event of a job loss due to voluntary reasons, such as old-age retirement, transfer to self-employment, disengagement due to marriage, childbirth and child rearing, continuing studies, and enlistment, the worker loses eligibility for unemployment benefits. By contrast, when a worker loses her/his job for involuntary reasons, such as redundancy, resignation at employers' suggestion, and honorary early retirement, the worker would be eligible to receive insurance benefits.

The aforementioned study aims to analyse whether female workers became involuntarily unemployed for fair and justifiable reasons vis-à-vis male workers. According to official statistics, male workers became involuntarily unemployed more often than female workers and therefore appear to have been more adversely affected by the crisis. The study argues, however, that absolute numbers of involuntary unemployment distort the more severe effects of the crisis on female versus male workers. The important numbers are each gender's relative shares of the 1998 involuntary unemployment among the respective total membership in the insurance scheme prior to the crisis in 1997. On the basis of an analysis of relative shares of both male and female involuntary unemployment by industry, occupation, age, educational attainment, and scale of enterprises, female workers disproportionately suffered from involuntary unemployment. These findings suggest that there must have been an extent of gender bias in the course of re-organizing firms and structural adjustment.

Between 1997 and 1998, the increase in the share of female involuntary unemployment among the total female members of the unemployment insurance system (24.7 per cent) was greater than that of male involuntary unemployment (19.4 per cent). This is particularly so in those cases where workers fell into involuntary unemployment because of reorganization redundancy, suggested resignation, and other types of dismissals. In this narrow sense of involuntary unemployment, females' share was about 16 per cent, compared with 12 per cent for male workers. Female workers must have been selected first, for involuntary retrenchment, and more for structural reorganization and redundancy.

53

4. Wages

According to the 1998 and 1997 Survey Reports on Wage Structures (Ministry of Labour 1999-1998), female workers' average compensation was only 61.7 per cent of male workers' average compensation in 1998. Although this is a slight improvement over 1997, when female workers' average compensation was 60.1 per cent that of the male workers, the gender gap in the average wage was substantial. Moreover, this gender gap in compensation was observed in all occupational groups.

Gender differences in compensation are also observed in the distribution of labour earnings. In 1998, while male workers with a low level of monthly compensation (below won 500,000 per month) were 1.3 per cent of the total male workers, as many as 6.6 per cent of female workers belonged to this low-level compensation group. Moreover, while male workers with a high level of total monthly compensation (above won 2 million) were 26.9 per cent of the total, only 5.5 per cent of female workers belonged to this group. The key issue is whether these compensation gaps between male and female workers come from gender differences in reasonable determinants of compensation (such as educational attainment, age and on-the-job experience, hours worked, etc.) or come more from gender bias.

As Kye (2000) points out, the impact of the Asian economic crisis on women in the Korean labour market can be summarized as follows:

- First, female labour force participation rates declined more drastically than male participation rates.

- Second, although female unemployment rates increased, male unemployment rates increased more sharply and reached a higher level than female unemployment rates.

- Third, when hidden unemployment is taken into account, female unemployment rates still stood higher than their male counterparts. However, the same trend was observed even before the crisis. Moreover, male unemployment rates rose faster than their female counterparts, and consequently females' share of total unemployment declined after the crisis erupted.

- Fourth, female workers with a lower level of education and with a job in female-dominated industries and occupations experienced unemployment in a greater proportion than their male counterparts, and some male workers replaced female workers in those industries and occupations.

- Fifth, unemployment spells were similar between male and female workers, and were even a bit shorter among female workers when hidden unemployment is considered.

- Sixth, the female employment level declined at a faster rate than male employment level, and female unemployed workers experienced a more rapid decline in re-employment rates.

- Seventh, when female unemployed workers were re-employed, they tended to get non-regular (daily) jobs more often than their male counterparts.

- Eighth, incidence of involuntary unemployment was higher among males than females; however, the relative share of involuntary unemployment in total unemployment insurance memberships of each gender group was greater among females, and they suffered more from enterprise reorganization and structural adjustment.

- Ninth, the average earnings of female workers were lower than those of their male counterparts.

From these findings, it is difficult to draw an unequivocal conclusion on whether female workers suffered more from the economic crisis or not since both male and female workers were adversely affected by the crisis. However, one can safely conclude that male and female workers were treated differently in the labour market, especially in terms of labour earnings, involuntary disengagement, and rehiring status. Some observers therefore argue that the differences in the effects of the economic crisis on men and women in the labour market originate from gender discrimination in the labour market.

One of the most striking aspects of the structure of women's employment is irregular employment. As of June 2000, only 47.1 per cent of all employed workers enjoyed "permanent employment". Temporary employees, with an employment contract of less than one year, and day labourers, with an employment contract of less than one month comprise 52.1 per cent of all employed workers. Notably, only 29.8 per cent of all employed women workers could be described as "permanently employed" while 46.2 per cent of women workers were temporary, and an additional 24.0 per cent were day labourers (KWWAU, 2000).

This phenomenon indicates the dismissal of full-time women workers and that any new openings for women were merely irregular work. Cho Soon-kyung (1999) analysing new openings in 17 banks and financial organizations in 1999 writes that only 10.8 per cent of the newly employed were given full-time positions and the rate of full-time women workers was 27.2 per cent. 90 per cent of the newly employed were on a temporary basis and out of this, 82 per cent were women workers.

Table III.2. Trends in employment status in the Republic of Korea, 1990-1999

(unit: per cent)

Year	Male employees				Female employees			
	Total	*Regular*	*Temporary*	*Casual*	*Total*	*Regular*	*Temporary*	*Casual*
1999	100.0	60.0	25.4	14.6	100.0	30.5	45.6	23.9
1998	100.0	64.8	23.4	11.8	100.0	34.1	47.8	18.1
1997	100.0	64.5	22.8	12.7	100.0	38.0	45.2	16.8
1996	100.0	66.7	21.0	12.3	100.0	40.7	43.1	16.2
1995	100.0	67.8	19.7	12.5	100.0	42.5	40.7	16.8
1994	100.0	67.6	19.7	12.7	100.0	42.0	40.8	17.2
1993	100.0	68.2	19.1	12.6	100.0	43.2	38.9	17.9
1992	100.0	66.6	20.3	13.0	100.0	41.1	39.8	19.0
1991	100.0	65.0	21.6	13.4	100.0	39.2	40.2	20.6
1990	100.0	64.5	22.4	13.1	100.0	37.6	39.6	22.8

Source: National Statistical Office (NS0, 1990-1999), *Annual Report on the Economically Active Population Survey*, each year.

B. Social protection and social safety nets

Table III.3 summarizes the measures for ensuring a minimum standard of living for Korean citizens. These include: 1) contributory social insurance schemes against the risks of old age, unemployment, industrial accident, sickness and maternity, and death; 2) public assistance programmes (includes ongoing and temporary schemes and related social services); and 3) indirect transfers to prevent families and individuals from falling into poverty, e.g. tax exemptions, subsidies for essential food items, subsidized health, education, day care services and public utilities, and other indirect transfers (Pak and others, 1999).

Table III.3. Social protection schemes in the Republic of Korea

	Programme	Social Risks Covered	Target Group	Status of Coverage
Social Insurance	National Pension	Old age	Wage workers and self employed	All industrial workers, self-employed
	Medical Insurance	Illness	All people	All permanent residents in Korea
	Industrial Accident Compensation Insurance	Industrial Accident	Wage workers	Workplaces under 5 employees, excluding temporary workers
	Employment Insurance	Unemployment	Wage workers	Excluding only daily workers (after October 1998)
Public Assistance	*Livelihood Protection (Self-reliance Protection)	Poverty	Low income group	Means tested
	Livelihood Protection (Home Protection)			Means tested

Source: Kim Mi Gon (reprinted from Pak Po-Hi and others, 1999).
    * The Livelihood Protection system was changed to the National Basic Livelihood Security system in 2000.

1. National pension

The national pension system was recently reformed to include coverage for divorced men and women (half of the pension benefits), and provides for women to postpone their contributions during maternity leave. However, under the current system, the enrolment for women is lower than that of men (table III.4). Moreover, for the majority of women, due to their relatively lower income, they face a higher risk of financial insecurity in their old age. Lower paying jobs generate lower benefit payments in payroll-dependent schemes; the gender disparity is aggravated by the persistent differential in women's earnings compared with those of male counterparts.

Table III.4. Pension enrolment and beneficiaries by sex in the Republic of Korea, 1996

Year	Sex	Nationwide		Nationwide	
		Enrolees	*Per cent*	*Beneficiaries*	*Per cent*
1996	Male	4 984 181	75.7	708 317	55.8
	Female	1 596 084	24.3	560 667	44.2
	Total	6 580 265	100.0	1 268 984	100.0

Source: Korean Women's Development Institute, *Statistical Yearbook on Women* (1999).

2. Medical insurance (National health insurance)

Since 1988, all Korean residents are covered by medical insurance, a programme that was recently changed to the National Health Insurance. However, coverage is still narrow and benefits are treatment-oriented. Notably, benefits pertinent to women's reproductive health need to be expanded.

3. Industrial accident compensation insurance

In 1998, the coverage of this insurance scheme was expanded to all workplaces, but the range of risks covered is still narrow and subject to frequent disputes between workers and management. In 1997, among 66,770 injured workers, 10.4 per cent were female. This small percentage may be explained by the fact that female workers, with marginal skills and resources, tend to be concentrated in risk-fraught small industries and are less likely to be protected by this insurance (Pak and others 1999).

4. Employment insurance

The Employment Insurance scheme was also expanded to cover all workplaces and, include both temporary and part-time workers; as of 1998, 72 per cent of waged workers were covered by this insurance scheme. In 1998, the unemployment rate for women was 5.6 per cent, and women were taking up a larger share of temporary and daily work. As of 1998, women accounted for 24 per cent of the total full-time workers, 55.4 per cent of temporary workers and 49.8 per cent of daily workers. This has serious implications for the receipt of unemployment benefits.

5. Public assistance

As shown in table III.5, women outnumber men as beneficiaries in public assistance schemes. In these programmes, 65 per cent of the Home Assistance beneficiaries and 38.4 per cent of the Self-reliance Assistance recipients are women aged 65 years and older. These statistics reflect the problems of feminization of poverty, and the issues of older women in the country.

Table III.5. Livelihood protection benefits by sex in the Republic of Korea, 1998

Year	Sex	Home Assistance		Self-Reliance Assistance	
		Number	*Per cent*	*Number*	*Per cent*
1998	Male	68 024	35.1	119 699	49.6
	Female	125 645	64.9	121 858	50.4
	Total	193 669	100.0	241 557	100.0

Source: Korean Women's Development Institute, *Statistical Yearbook on Women* (1999).

With the enactment of the National Basic Livelihood Security Law in 1999, the system of the previous Livelihood Protection was changed to (i) enhance the rights to claim, (ii) abolish the demographic eligibility criteria, (iii) achieve equity by introducing the concept of Estimated Household Income and, (iv) enhance the productivity of the welfare system by providing the unemployed with incentives and systematic self-support programmes (Kim 2001). However, problems still persist and chief among them is the question of monitoring the effectiveness and efficiency of this revised system, especially in terms of its gender responsiveness.

6. Social services for women

The Ministry of Health and Welfare provides social services to children, people with disabilities, older people and women in separate delivery systems. With the establishment of the Ministry of Gender Equality, services for the victims of violence against women will be funded and operated by this Ministry. The social services to help women overcome various crises, as well as to support their social participation, include the following:

- services for women at-risk, for example unwed mothers, single mothers, runaway women, victims of domestic and sexual violence, prostitution, etc.

- services to support balancing work and family, for example, daycare for children/ people with disabilities and the elderly/ after-school programmes.

- services and programmes for education and social activity, for example, skills training, cultural programmes, social education, volunteer programmes, etc.

Table III.6. Social services for women at risk, Republic of Korea

Type of facility	Number of facilities	Number of clients	Target group	Services and programmes	Time of care (extended care)
Single Mother's Housing	37	2 620	low-income single mother families with children under the age of 18 who do not have housing protection	– free housing – living expenses – tuition support for children – resettlement fund	3 years (2 years)

(continued)

Table III.6 *(continued)*

Type of facility	Number of facilities	Number of clients	Target group	Services and programmes	Time of care (extended care)
Single Mother's Temporary Shelter	6	275	victims of domestic violence	– free housing and food – job training	2 month (1 month)
Unwed-Mother's Shelter	8	226	unwed pregnant women	– free housing and food – support for delivery – job training	6 months
Guidance and Protection Facility	21	275	prostitutes and runaway women	– free housing and food – counselling – job training	6 months (6 months)
Victims of Sexual Violence Shelter	6	26	victims of sexual violence	– free housing and food – counselling and treatment	6 months (1 month)
Victims of Domestic Violence Shelter	15	124	victims of domestic violence	– free housing and food – counselling and treatment	2 months (1 month)
Sexual Violence Counselling Centres	62		victims of sexual violence	– counselling, information and referral	
Domestic Violence Counselling Centres	133		victims of domestic violence	– counselling, information and referral	

Source: *Guideline for Social Services for Women* (Ministry of Health and Welfare, 2000).

7. Special policies and programmes for women

With the onset of the economic crisis, the Government developed various policies and programmes to alleviate its impact. Table III.7 summarizes the schemes implemented by the Government and non-governmental agencies to help women meet the challenges of unemployment and poverty.

Table III.7. Policies for unemployed women in the Republic of Korea

Unemployment Policies	Policies Targeted at Women
Active labour market policies Measures to minimize unemployment Creation of new jobs	Establishment of a reporting system on discriminatory lay offs Participation of female representatives in the lay off process Incentives for employment of female heads of households Finance hotline called 'Equality Hotline' Inclusion of women-friendly public works Increase the ratio of female public works participants Business loans for female household heads

(continued)

59

Table III.7 *(continued)*

Unemployment Policies	*Policies Targeted at Women*
Protection of and support for the unemployed	Opening of part time job referral centres
Speedy job referral	Job referrals for college graduate women
Job training	Job fairs for women
Financial support	Develop jobs for re-entry women
	Special Job training for female household heads
	Expansion of working women's centres
	Increase women's job training
	Expand Employment Insurance
	Income assistance for low-income families
	Loans
	Social services to prevent family breakdown
	Child care support for the unemployed

Source: Kim and Moon, *The Current Status of Unemployed Women and Policies* (Korean Women's Development Institute, 1999).

In order to meet the needs of unemployed women suffering from the impact of the economic crisis in the late 1990s, the Ministry of Labour, together with the Presidential Commission on Women's Affairs took a relatively proactive role in developing schemes to respond to the special needs of women. While various active labour market policies were successful in preventing some discriminatory practices of companies, they could not prevent the worsening of women's working conditions. More recently, there has been policy debates on expanding day care services and socializing maternity protection measures in order to achieve more significant results for women vis-à-vis access to labour markets.

In 1998, special divisions for women's policies were established in six different Government Ministries in the Republic of Korea – the Ministries of Justice, Government Administration and Home Affairs, Education, Agriculture and Forestry, Health and Welfare, and Labour – along with local government agencies on women to coordinate and implement women's policies in diverse sectors. In 2000, the Ministry of Gender Equality was established to develop and implement various national policies to advance the status of women and to achieve gender equal society. Gender mainstreaming is a key objective in each Ministry and local Governments.

The Ministry of Gender Equality has a comprehensive plan to prevent unemployment of women, and to increase women's economic activities. The Ministry will evaluate employers regarding their hiring practices, implement a mentoring programme for prospective business owners and female entrepreneurs, expand market opportunities for products of women-owned businesses, set up job searching services for new female college graduates, expand women-friendly training programmes, and prepare guidelines for the implementation of the Basic Labour Act for temporary workers.

Moreover, the Ministry plans to redesign the programmes of the Working Women's Centres so that they can respond more effectively to the market needs of local communities, and to increase the capacity of women vis-à-vis information technology and other professional requirements. There are currently 46 Working Women's Centres throughout the country, and they have trained 27,637 women in the year 2000 with a 47 per cent success in job placements.

Women's NGOs have also been active in alleviating the problems of women's unemployment. They engaged in advocacy of the seriousness of the issues, as well as designed and implemented women-friendly public works programmes with the assistance of government funding. Some NGOs also operate information and referral services for job-seeking women, operate Working Women's Centres, and develop support networks. They also advocate for the rights of temporary workers, that they be included in the social security system, and campaign for the revision of public assistance, socialization of maternity protection cost, etc.

C. A gender evaluation of the social safety nets responding to the needs of women during the crisis

Looking at the public works programmes, there were 74,777 beneficiaries who participated in the first round of these projects in 1998. However, women were seriously limited in opportunities to participate in the first round of the public works projects. This was because the recipients of the projects were limited to the heads of households or the main breadwinners, which in the Republic of Korea consists mainly of men, and consequently in the beginning only 32.3 per cent of the participants were women. As a result of women's protests, eligibility requirements were relaxed and additional projects for women such as women's welfare assistants and after-school instructor positions were expanded. Consequently, women's participation increased to a little over 50 per cent. The programmes that saw the greatest participation by women were the public service works and environmental pro-grammes. Women worked as teachers in after-school programmes for children of low-income families, helpers in social services, and office assistants in university libraries and Government offices. Although these later public works programmes received some positive evaluations, setbacks included a lack of job continuity, enthusiasm for the work (motivation), and choice.

According to the Korean Women Workers Associations United, women were excluded as recipients in other policies as well (KWWAU 2000). Unemployment benefits, which are supposed to benefit all the unemployed, were heavily in favour of men. Out of a total of 8,082 cases amounting to 50.5 billion won, men constituted 7,725 cases (95.6 per cent) receiving 48.5 billion won (96 per cent), and women's cases numbered 357 (4.4 per cent) receiving only 4 per cent of the budget. The reason again is because eligibility was restricted to heads of households and/or primary income earners of the family. Generally, even when women are responsible for the livelihood of a family, she is not legally considered the head of household or the primary income earner, if there is a husband living in the house. An ILO report explained that, in addition to women being primarily represented in low skill jobs and in hardest hit sectors, women often bore the brunt of retrenchment by firms because they were not perceived as primary breadwinners, and therefore, had other forms of support. This view, however, does not reflect the reality. In the Republic of Korea, women head 16 per cent of all households.

Policies that reflect bias towards men, as heads of household and primary income earners, were evident in job training programmes. Job training for women, for instance, included beauty schools, cooking schools, baking classes, design schools, etc, which have traditionally been occupations held by women. These training programmes require a short learning period and simple skills, with little future prospects and placement in jobs with relatively lower wages (Jang 1998). This is consistent with policy that worked to incorporate the female labour force into the general labour market as a low-wage menial labour force. Such job training programmes failed to take into consideration the demands in the labour market for such skills, and does not have provisions to find employment after training.

There is evidence that, the number of cases of employers dismissing employees because of marriage or pregnancy had also increased despite pro-women labour market policies put in place by the Government. According to the "Equality Hotline" of the KWWAU, the number of counselling cases received in 1999 relating to maternal leave has risen to three times that of 1998, which reflected the employment practices such as dismissals because of pregnancy and childbirth. This reflects the regression of maternal protection under the pretence of the economic crisis.

Middle-aged women were especially unaffected by whatever pro-women labour market policies; they continued to face increasing difficulties in re-employment. Unemployed middle-aged women who had registered at the Action Centre for Unemployment Women of KWWAU in 1999 even stated their willingness to accept any type of job placements (KWWAU 2000). According to an analysis on the characteristics of unemployed women in their forties and sixties seeking employment (Pak and others 1999), there was a 100,000 won gap in wages women were willing to receive before and after their dismissals.

D. Conclusions

Social protection policies and programmes, to meet the needs of women in the context of the crisis has been quite successful to a certain extent, but the globalization of the world economy, demographic trends and other factors have placed many women in a disadvantaged and vulnerable position.

Although it was not possible to state unequivocally that female workers were more adversely affected by the Asian crisis, there is no doubt that female workers were acutely affected by the crisis. Moreover, female workers have gone through a labour market experience different from that of male workers, especially in the fields of hidden unemployment, the speed of unemployment, re-employment status, concentration, incidence of involuntary disengagement, and labour earnings. Therefore, during an economic recession or crisis, the Government may want to take a series of special measures focused on tackling female workers' problems and issues, separately from the general approach taken for all workers. Those measures may include labour market information systems with special emphasis on monitoring female workers' situation, special job counselling for women so as to help them stay in the market and search for a job actively, special employment service and training programmes and facilities for female workers, and a reinforced labour inspection system with a focus on motherhood protection.

Despite the setting up of special divisions for women, a new Ministry and reforms in gender-related laws and policies, these have had but a limited impact in improving the situation of women in the country. Women in the Republic of Korea remain a vulnerable social group in many respects. In the sphere of social reproduction, women are not equal partners in the family; they have less access to employment opportunities as compared to their male counterparts; they are frequently subject to physical, mental and sexual abuses and/or violence in and out of the domestic context; they do not enjoy equal access to socio-economic development resources; and the current legal and judicial provisions and practices are not entirely adequate in protecting them.

CHAPTER IV.

THAILAND

The Asian financial and economic crisis affected people in Thailand, in a more or less similar fashion as it happened in other crisis-hit countries. The initial capital flight triggered a currency depreciation, domestic credit shortages, widespread corporate financial difficulties and severe contractions in demand and output. In addition, the second round of contagion effects led to a fall in export demand (through the depreciation of other currencies), which exerted a further drag on income and output. Consequently, these mechanisms led to further drops in employment and wages as well as lower government revenues and budgets for a number of social programmes. Additionally, local currency depreciation affects the earnings of tradable sectors and, eventually, the poor are hit with increases in costs of living.

The crisis in Thailand, as elsewhere, had also a clear gendered dimension in terms of its social impacts. Not only did women and girls suffer disproportionately in the effects of the crisis, but there is also ample evidence that women played a major role in managing the response to economic shocks at the household and often the community level. It is they who made the decisions, such as food expenditures, on which the survival of the household is based, and they also actively strategized to increase household incomes in activities such as joining the informal sector by selling goods.

The Government of Thailand initially responded to the onset of the crisis by increasing public expenditures across the board in 1997. But 1998 brought an inflation-adjusted budget reduction and, therefore, affected social programmes to mitigate the shocks of the crisis on poor households. Multilateral and bilateral financial assistance extended loans to help cover Thailand's balance of payments shortfall and support the budgets of existing health, education, and environmental protection projects, as well as fund a number of social safety net programmes.

How effective were these programmes? Were they designed to reflect the gender realities of the country's labour markets and social structures? This chapter examines the social impacts of the crisis in Thailand, the social protection programmes that existed prior to the crisis and those put in place at the onset of the crisis. Of special concern is the impact of the crisis as well as the social protection programmes on the situation of women in the country.

A. Social impacts of the crisis

The financial crisis resulted in a steep decline in investment. With the devaluation of the Thai currency of between 40 to 50 per cent, the rate of inflation increased from 5.5 per cent in 1997 to 8.1 per cent in 1998. The inflationary pressure subsided because of the contraction of demand.

The impact of economic crisis was clearly evident in the growth rate, especially in 1998, when it plunged to –9.4 per cent. The industrial sector was the hardest hit, the rate of growth falling to –12.5 per cent, and –8.3 per cent in the service sector. In comparison, the agricultural sector was less affected with a growth rate of –0.4 per cent.

The devaluation of the baht did not lead to an increase in the value of exports as was expected. In 1997, the value of exports increased by 4.8 per cent but in 1998, the rate of increase was –7.6 per cent. In 1999, exports increased by 3.2 per cent. Devaluation of the local currency made imports more expensive, raising the rate of imports by 15.7 per cent. With the fall in aggregate demand, the rate of imports amounted to –32.1 per cent in 1998 (table IV.1).

1. Employment, 1997-1999

Soon after the crisis hit the country, the Government adopted an austerity programme characterized by deflationist measures such as high interest rates and budget cuts. The high interest rate, credit crunch and contraction of the market pushed the economy into a recession substantially faster and deeper than expected. The bankruptcies of small and medium enterprises (SMEs), which represented the backbone of the country's industries, led to massive retrenchment of workers. In Thailand in 1995, SMEs accounted for 90 percent of total registered businesses, employing 73.8 percent of the total work force (Praparpun 1999: 126). The slump in the real estate sector had earlier already generated a massive unemployment in the construction sector. And unemployment worsened, as white-collar workers were laid-off with closures of banks and other financial institutions.

The immediate social impact of the crisis was the 30,270 unemployed persons in 1998 as compared to 31,710 persons in 1997. Employment in the non-agricultural sector decreased from 17,400 persons to 16,700 in 1998. Unemployment was estimated at 1.42 million or 4.4 per cent of the labour force in 1998. In June 1999, unemployment declined to 1.38 million or 4.2 per cent of the labour force (table IV.2).

The third round of Labour Force Status (LFS), conducted in August 1997, showed no effects of the crisis on employment. Indeed, employment was up and unemployment was down by over 50 per cent. Employment began to decline, in the next LFS round of February 1998. There was a year-on-year decline of 2.8 per cent followed by another 3.1 per cent year-on-year decline in the third quarter of 1998. In terms of absolute numbers, employment had declined by about a million persons from the earlier year levels in the third quarter of 1998. In the third quarter of 1999, employment started increasing again before another decline in early 2000.

The percentage increases in unemployment was significantly higher than the corresponding decrease in employment. This was because of high growth rates during the early 1990s, when unemployment rates were very low. With the onset of the crisis, the unemployment rate skyrocketed from a low level of 0.9 per cent in August 1997 to 3.4 per cent in August 1998. By the third-quarter of 1999, unemployment levels began to fall but picked up again in the first quarter of 2000.

Table IV.1. Economic growth in Thailand, 1997-1999

	1997	*1998*	*1999*
Exchange Rate	31.37	41.37	38.00
Real GDP growth			
Agriculture	−0.10	−0.40	1.80
Industry	−0.50	−12.50	3.80
Service	−2.10	−8.30	1.60
Total	−1.30	−9.40	2.50
CIP			
Growth	5.50	8.10	1.10
Average price index	118.20	127.80	154.60
Total investment	−23.00	−30.60	4.50
Export			
Value (US$ billion)	57.05	52.72	54.50
percentage change	4.80	−7.60	3.20
Import			
Value (US$ billion)	59.75	40.56	44.10
percentage change	−15.70	−32.10	8.00
Trade balance			
Value (US$ billion)	−2.70	12.16	10.41

Source: Thailand Development Research Institute (September 1999).

Table IV.2. Population, employment and unemployment in Thailand, 1997-1999

	1997	*1998*	*1999*
Population (million)	60.82	61.47	62.08
(at year end)			
Labour force	32.78	32.6	32.91
(13 year of age and over)	(1.4)	(−0.6)	(1.0)
Employed	31.71	30.27	30.84
	(1.8)	(−4.6	(1.9)
Agriculture	14.32	13.57	14.00
	(1.3)	(−5.2)	(3.1)
Non-agriculture	17.40	16.70	16.84
	(2.2)	(−4.0)	(0.8)
Unemployed persons	0.50	1.42	1.38
(as per cent of labour force)	(1.5)	(4.4)	(4.2)
Open unemployment	(0.4)	(1.4)	(1.2)
Passive unemployment	(1.1)	(3.0)	(3.0)
Seasonal inactive labour force	0.57	0.90	0.69
(as percentage of labour force)	(1.7)	(2.8)	(2.1)

Source: Key Economic Indicators, (Bank of Thailand, 28 April 2000).

2. Unemployment and retrenchment

In 1998, employment in construction in rural areas fell to 0.8 million as compared to 1.4 million in the previous year, whereas in urban areas it fell from 0.6 million persons in 1997 to 0.44 million persons in 1998 and 0.37 million in 1999. There was also the unemployment of new entrants to the labour market, unable to find employment. The major cause of the dramatic unemployment was due to lay-offs in factories. In 1997, almost half of the unemployed were those laid off from factories unable to cope with the crisis (table IV.3).

Statistics of reported cases on labour disputes and from factory inspections show that the financial sector and real estate had the highest number of lay-offs (table IV.4). In the textile industry, the number of lay-offs was also high but this was a problem that had begun before the crisis. In 1998, the number of women workers laid-off was higher than men. The industries with the highest number of retrenched workers were textile and garment and electronics, where women comprised 80 to 90 per cent of the workforce. The devaluation of the currency was expected to boost exports of products from these labour-intensive industries. This did not happen.

Table IV.3. Number of establishments, employees and lay-offs, Thailand, 1997-1999

Year	Number of Establishments		Number of Employees	
	Total	*Lay-off / Temporary or closed down*	*Total*	*Number of Lay-off*
1997	339 001	4 941	7 690 700	408 967
1998	331 425	5 827	6 250 307	355 628
1999	337 088	4 484	6 451 833	84 415

Source: Department of Labour Protection and Welfare, Thailand.

Table IV.4. Number of lay-offs classified by sectors and sex, Thailand, 1997-1998

Type	Number of Establishments		Number of Lay-offs					
			Total		*Men*		*Women*	
	1997	*1998*	*1997*	*1998*	*1997*	*1998*	*1997*	*1998*
1. Garment	16	22	1 590	3 485	617	261	973	3 224
2. Textile	25	18	4 309	8 147	1 025	1 195	3 014	6 952
3. Footwear and leather	14	11	1 423	1 007	431	193	992	814
4. Toys	8	7	600	1 087	86	118	514	969
5. Canned, frozen food	19	50	2 622	1 491	827	664	1 795	820
6. Jewellery	12	9	671	258	327	34	344	224
7. Finance	77	48	5 111	2 005	2 207	843	2 904	1 162

(continued)

Table IV.4 *(continued)*

Type	Number of Establishments		Number of Lay-offs					
			Total		Men		Women	
	1997	*1998*	*1997*	*1998*	*1997*	*1998*	*1997*	*1998*
8. Furniture	36	19	2 623	827	2 052	454	571	373
9. Electric and electronic	32	76	3 500	6 080	1 257	1 690	2 243	4 386
10. Spareparts-motorcycles	73	57	3 551	4 881	2 724	3 954	827	927
11. Iron and steel	25	49	892	2 244	727	1 799	165	445
12. Servicing	90	125	1 678	1 816	905	825	773	991
13. Printing and advertising	16	18	838	803	440	410	398	393
14. Real estate	138	100	4 495	2 765	3 305	2 190	1 190	575
15. Supermarket-mini mart	28	6	1 733	245	524	82	1 209	163
16. Transport	12	44	98	945	80	669	18	275
17. Concrete products	38	34	1 940	2 587	1 350	1 786	590	801
18. Retail trade	95	221	1 178	1 876	618	1 088	560	790
19. Others	149	135	6 173	7 948	3 505	3 126	2 668	4 822
Total	903	1 049	45 025	50 497	23 007	21 381	21 748	29 106

Source: Statistics collected from cases reported on labour disputes and from factory inspections, Department of Protection and Welfare, Thailand.

3. Working hours and wages

One other impact of the crisis was in the reduction in work hours. It appeared that this was more pronounced in the rural areas as shown previously in Table I.10. This may be because as more retrenched workers returned to the countryside, more persons shared farm work and incomes. In Thailand, the relatively larger smallholder-agriculture sector appears to have acted as a shock absorber, leading to smaller increases in open unemployment in the country. This demonstrates the well-integrated rural and urban labour markets in Thailand, which also explains the widely distributed drop in wages, and the increase in rural poverty, where many unemployed migrants sought work. Changes in the patterns of internal migration during the crisis were significant.

Labour demand shocks also hurt households through lower real wages. Average wages in manufacturing fell and fluctuated. This was so because factories were employing more workers on a temporary or short-term contract work basis at lower wages than existing permanent employees.

4. Unemployment and the impact on women workers

The economic crisis hit households adversely through falling labour demand, sharp price shifts, a public spending squeeze and an erosion of the social fabric. All these caused female layoffs, their real wage declines, weak demand for new labour market entrants and massive entries into the informal sector. As discussed earlier, employment earlier on in the crisis declined sharply and this decline affected more women than men. The number of persons, reported as being retrenched in 1997, was 44,753 persons. Of this number, there was a slightly higher proportion of women workers. In 1998, however, there was a much larger number of women laid off; 29,106 women workers were laid-off in 1998 compared to 21,381 the previous year. According to a survey by the Arom Pongpangan Foundation Labour Resource Centre, 60 per cent of the workers who lost jobs in Thailand were women over 30 years of age, one quarter of whom had been textile and garment workers. Production workers were not the only ones affected; about 200,000 white-collar workers mainly from the finance and banking sectors also lost their jobs, many of them women.

According to the aforementioned survey, women experienced difficulties in finding new jobs because of old age, lack of new skills and low education. Most of the laid off women workers were aged 40 to 50 or near retirement. It appeared that employers chose to retrench the more senior workers in order to avoid paying retirement benefits and other emoluments associated with seniority. Many found it difficult to find new jobs or did not hope to find new jobs, as their qualifications did not match current requirements.

With no employment and a rising cost of living, the consumption pattern of many households was affected, including housing and the education of children. Additionally, in the face of these hardships, many became indebted to informal moneylenders. In cases where both husband and wife lost their jobs, the responsibility of maintaining the family fell on women's shoulders. The survey also noted that women tend to take more initiative in seeking new jobs, while unemployed men often tend to be easily discouraged.

Employment is an essential means to income, nutrition, health, and education, as well as to the less tangible but no less important attribute of self-esteem. The impact of rising unemployment had affected women in some households more than others and thus altered the income distribution and led to a lowering of living standards. Price increases for basic foodstuffs also affected consumption patterns – particularly for women and children. According to a UNDP study (2000), food makes up a relatively large share of Thailand's poor people's consumption basket. For the average poor household, food accounts for 55 per cent of household expenditure Thus, the impact on women's living standard vis-à-vis the significant price increases for food was relatively large in the country for the existing poor families.

Cases were reported of firms using the crisis as an excuse to lay off workers. And in many instances, legal compensation was not paid and workers were forced to take the dispute to the labour court. Workers also faced union busting, increased casualization of work and insecure subcontracting work. Again, these features increasingly characterized the status of women as workers during the crisis.

In Thailand, as elsewhere, the flexibility of women's labour is associated with the casualization of labour – for example, part-time work, piece-rate contracts, subcontracting and home-based work. According to the results of a recent special survey of home workers, a total of 311,790 people were home workers in Thailand in 1999. Most home workers were females. Of all the 311,790 home workers, 20.0 per cent were males and 80.0 per cent were females. They worked at home or in the nearby area, so that they could at the same time look after the family or do household chores, which matched the role of women. This is rooted in the gender division of labour in everyday life, such that women are allocated the responsibility of caring for the dependent members of the community – the young, the old, the sick and those with disabilities. Because of their gender role in society, women tend to enter the workforce with a propensity to seek casualized forms of employment that would enable them to combine their income-earning activities with their caring activities.

The aftermath of the crisis saw a resurgence of localism as a "political response" to the crisis. Connors (2001) notes that the key principle of localism is to root development in local communities, which are seen as having the capacity to be self-reliant and self-sustaining. In Thailand, the discourse of localism, which first arose in the late 1970s, came to be known as watthanatham chumchon or "community culture". Following the crisis, the notion of self-reliant and self-sustaining communities was valorised as the ideal type on which to re-organize the whole of society and economy. (See Phongpaichit and Baker, 2000, pp. 195-199).

Many women moved into informal sector employment, making a living in petty trade. A survey by the National Statistical Organisation (1997) found that 80 percent of those employed in petty trade and commerce worked in the informal labour market. One group of women, laid off by a garment factory pooled their money and skills together to set up a small garment-manufacturing network. These small informal subcontractors were able to make a living in a time of crisis, but their situation remained precarious. Their problems reflected the situation of informal workers everywhere – lack of access to credit, lack of skills and irregular, insecure working conditions.

Women workers who experienced work-related health problems are laid-off and, if they do not have a financial support system to fall back on, will join the category of the poor. For many, the alternative is to engage in petty trade in the informal sector. Because of their illness, however, they faced even more difficulties on top of the usual problems of informal workers.

Many of the displaced women who joined the ranks of those who work in the informal sector also took up sex work. Because of such livelihood difficulties, many turned to sex work as a major coping strategy. Figures on women and girls involved in sex work are difficult to obtain. Prior to the economic crisis of 1997, significant numbers were already involved in the sex industry. In Thailand, a Ministry of Public Health survey recorded 65,000 prostitutes in 1997 but unofficial sources put the figure at a much higher level. There are also thousands of Thai prostitutes working in other countries. It is also estimated that close to US$300 million is transferred annually to rural families by Thai women working in the sex sector in urban areas (Son 1998).

The Ministry of Education estimated that in Thailand there were half a million children who had dropped out of school during the crisis years. Another report by End Child Prostitution in Asian Tourism Initiative stated that there has been a 10 per cent decrease in school enrolment at primary school level in Thailand since 1996. Due to increased unemployment, children also moved to the informal labour market and were also vulnerable to sexual exploitation. The same report suggested that a great number of children were known to travel to tourist areas and to big cities hoping to find work (ECPAT 1998).

B. Social protection and social safety nets

1. The Miyazawa Plan and the Social Investment Project

Initial measures adopted by the Government to address the impacts of the economic crisis such as the reduction of budget deficit, the tight monetary policy and high interest rates had led to a general contraction of the economy. What began as a recession of the economy was turned into a deep depression resulting in a steep fall in economic growth. This led the Government to adopt a policy of employment creation as its first priority to mitigate the shocks of crisis. And employment was to be generated through expenditure measures, designed to target those affected by the crisis in both rural and urban areas.

External borrowing financed these expenditure measures. The Miyazawa Plan amounted to US$ 1.45 billion, World Bank funding amounted to US$ 600 million, the Japan Exim Bank financed another US$ 600 million, and US$ 250 million came from the OECF. The objective was to use these funds to stimulate the economy through job creation and productive investments, while at the same time cushioning the poor from the crisis.

Under the Miyazawa Plan, funds would be channelled through government ministries, from the central to the provincial and district levels. Each district will be allotted 100,000 baht to be spent on job-creation ranging from reservoir digging, clearing drainage and constructing earth-filled roads. The District Administrative Council will be responsible for overseeing the employment of the beneficiaries and monitoring these public work programmes.

In addition to the Miyazawa package, the Social Investment Project (SIP), co-financed by the Government, the World Bank, OECF, UNDP and AusAID to a total amount of $ 450 million, was put in place in 1998. One component of the SIP involved supporting existing Government programmes aimed at providing jobs to the unemployed and the poor. These employment creation programmes were entrusted to the Ministry of Labour and Social Welfare, Ministry of Interior, Bangkok Metropolitan Administration, Tourism Authority of Thailand and the Royal Irrigation Department of the Ministry of Agriculture and Coopera-tives. Most of these programmes involved creating jobs through the implementation of small-scale public works intended for a target group of two million unemployed persons.

The Government also allocated a portion of the World Bank loan to social investments in community development funds. Two funds were set up: the "Social Investment Fund" (SIF) for local and community grassroots organizations to implement their development projects and the National Economic and Social Development Board's (NESDB) Regional Urban Development Fund (RUDF), a revolving fund to be channelled to municipalities for capital investment projects. These programmes would be managed under an innovative "bottom-up" system. The new system will provide for funds to be allocated from the top down, as has been case in the past, but facilitated through the Social Fund Office (SOFO) of the Government Saving Bank. The SOFO, managed by ex-NGO personnel, would provide grants for projects, which are aimed at strengthening community organizations.

The SIF was targeted at projects initiated by local community organizations, municipali-ties, and other informal groups such as cooperatives, women groups, environmental protection groups or groups associated with the temples and schools. SIF projects are supposed to promote "civil society" all over the country and "good governance" at different levels.

During the initial phase, SIF investments covered four main categories. They are (i) Community Economy, which includes community demonstrations and learning centres, community markets, training in production and marketing of products and community water supply; (ii) Community Welfare and Safety, which finances community child development and day care centres, playgrounds and shelters for the elderly and HIV/AIDS patients; (iii) Natural Resource Management and Cultural Presentation, which includes mangrove preservation, forestry management and cultural preservation activities; and (iv) Community Capacity Building and Networking, which covers activities in community network development, occupation development and saving group capacity development. In March 1999, the SIF proposed additional projects that would qualify for eligibility. This category was Emergency Community Welfare, designed to finance immediate community welfare assistance needs arising from the crisis. The objective of this programme is to respond to the urgent needs of poor communities and the increasing demands on organizations struggling to assist them. The new window will finance social assistance transfers through community organization networks to those most vulnerable; thereby strengthening the coping capacities of groups most severely affected by the crisis

2. Measures to counter unemployment

In July 1997, the Ministry of Labour and Social Welfare (MOLSW) set up the Centre for Assistance to Laid-Off workers (CALOW), which would act as "one-stop" services centres providing training, referrals, counselling and placement services. The centres' activities are funded by an ADB loan. The centre will collect data and information on lay-offs and unemployment and study, analyse and propose measures to counter the problem. It will also cooperate with other departments to help laid-off workers.

The Government implemented both short- and long-term measures to counter the unemployment situation.

The short-term measures included:

1) Monitoring of labour market information. The MOLSW would cooperate with other ministries such as the Ministry of Commerce, Ministry of Industry, Board of Investment (BOI), and the NESDB in order to analyse and evaluate the business situation in order to obtain accurate numbers of laid-off workers; 2) cooperate with employers so that laid-off workers would obtain compensation such as severance payments, wages etc., according to labour protection laws; 3) find new placements for unemployed persons; 4) provide training referrals and, 5) Consult with the Ministry of Agriculture and Cooperatives, the Ministry of Industry, and the Ministry of Education, for the purpose of retraining and seeking other funding sources.

The long-term measures included:

1) Concentrating in labour-skills training of industrial technicians, which are in great demand; 2) training in services skills such as housekeeping, driving, and cooking for the hotel industry; and 3) creating of employment opportunities in rural areas.

In June 1997, the MOLSW sought cooperation from employers for its programme entitled "Remedy Measures for Lay-offs". This programme is characterized by: 1) cost-saving by management before implementing cost reduction measures that reduced labour demand; 2) employment-reduction measures to be done after new recruitment is terminated; existing workers should be given priority when there are new vacancies; wages and other benefits will not be compromised when workers are transferred from one position to another; early retirement should be on voluntary basis; and termination of contracts should be targeted at those who are the most recently recruited, have unfavourable work records and work ethics.

In September 1997, the MOLSW had devised a system of reporting on lay-offs and unemployment. At the provincial level, the labour welfare and protection officer would have access to the social welfare officer in the same province to obtain a list of enterprises at which lay-offs occur to verify the number of laid-off employees and assist them in obtaining compensation in line with labour laws. The proposed compensation would then be submitted to the provincial governor, director general, and CALOW as well as to the respective labour officers at the provincial level (to inform of vacancies, job application forms, training application forms, as well as new recruitment at the lay-off site), to social welfare (for the issuance of medical cards), to the directors of skill development centres (for referral training, skill development or new placement training), to public welfare (to provide minimum assistance) and to the office of the permanent.

In December 1997, the MOLSW drafted another action plan to address lay-offs and unemployment. This programme included measures aimed at: 1) cost savings on the part of employers and employees such as temporary work holidays, overtime work, shorter working hours, wage reductions and early retirement; 2) enhancing labour relations by being transparent to labour unions on all mitigating measures; 3) addressing liquidity problems of firms by gathering relevant information of affected enterprises to inform the Ministry of Finance and the Bank of Thailand.

Other measures to mitigate unemployment shocks in the short-term included: 1) Thais assisting Thais by organizing caravans selling affordable consumer goods and setting up funds to assist the self-employed; 2) ministries adjusting their budgets to generate rural employment; 3) repatriation of illegal, foreign workers; 4) promoting of Thai labour emigration; 5) promotion of employment in the industrial sector with various measures such as cost savings, marketing promotion, recruiting of laid-off persons, skills development for new technologies, investment opportunities in agriculture and promotion of self-employed businesses; 6) self-reliance and self-sufficiency in agriculture; 7) assistance to newly graduated students seeking employment and providing educational support to the unemployed; 8) encouraging the community and the unemployed to accept subcontract works from the Bangkok Metropolitan Authority; and 9) encouraging those with education to take up temporary employment under the coordination of the NESDB.

Additionally, the Government responded to labour demand shocks in four main ways. First, it extended the severance pay requirements from 6 to 10 months (for employees with more than 10 years working experience) and established a fund to pay severance payments to workers whose firms had gone bankrupt. Second, the Government extended social security benefits to laid-off subscribers from 6 to 12 months and the tripartite contribution rate for such benefits was reduced by one-third. Third, a major job-creation programme in rural areas was launched in March 1999 and continued in 2000 in order to absorb returning migrants. Fourth, training programmes were launched to upgrade the skills of workers laid off during the crisis, through free short-term vocational and technical training with subsequent job placements.

C. A gender evaluation of the crisis-initiated social safety nets

The Miyazawa package provided employment to 88,967 educated employees and another 3.5 million workers were employed an average of 18 days which is equivalent to 319,182 person years. The various SIP employment generating projects created employment opportunities for about 170,000 workers (World Bank 2000c). With such a large number of beneficiaries, one would expect the impact of the job creation programmes to show up in reduced unemployment numbers for the country in mid to late 1999. An examination of the August round of the Labour Force Survey (LFS) 1999 shows that unemployment in Thailand fell from 1.14 million persons in August 1998 to 0.99 million in August 1999 – a decline of nearly 14 per cent year on year. This was the first such decline in unemployment year-on-year since the onset of the crisis. In fact, unemployment had been increasing earlier in that year. For example, between February 1998 and February 1999, unemployment had gone up from 1.5 million persons to 1.7 million persons – an increase of over 13 per cent. From this, therefore, the World Bank concluded that the statistics confirmed that the declining trend in unemployment was a result of the employment generation programmes. "Of course, it is unlikely that the Miyazawa package accounted for all of the decline in unemployment in August 1999. The improving economy and other employment generation programmes also likely contributed to the decline in unemployment" (World Bank 2000c).

1. Survey findings on the implementation of employment/income generating projects to alleviate the economic crisis impacts on Thailand

In 1999, ESCAP launched a research project aimed at evaluating various Government policies and programs implemented to alleviate the socio-economic costs of rising unemployment and loss of income associated with the Asian economic crisis. The project involved surveys and in-depth analyses at institutional and beneficiary levels to assess the effectiveness of income and employment generating programs in the main crisis-hit countries, including Thailand. The main objectives of the surveys were to identify and evaluate whether or not gender issues were attended to in the design and implementation of the social safety net policies and programs. In other words, if safety net policies are to be effective, they will have to reflect the social and economic conditions of women.

The target population for the interviews, in Thailand, was set at 250 for public works programmes (PWP) and 250 for microcredit programmes (MCP). To obtain the samples, the sites of the fieldwork were chosen according to criteria such as types of programmes, number of beneficiaries participated, areas affected and active NGO collaboration with the targeted population in order to get access to information.

For PWP, two provinces were selected. One was Surin, the lower north-eastern province characterized by populations with low per capita incomes and many out-migrant workers. As for the interviewees, they consisted of the beneficiaries of the Miyazawa programme. The beneficiaries included retrenched workers who migrated back to the countryside since the crisis erupted 1997. Other interviewees were small-scale rice farmers, who also earned additional income from off-farm activities. The Miyazawa-funded PWP involved small projects such as dredging, well-digging and road construction.

The second site chosen for the PWP interviews was Viang Nong Long district, Lumpoon province in the northern region. 150 interviews were conducted using structured questionnaires and participant observation notes were also recorded.

250 interviews were conducted for the MCP. The sites selected were Bangkok and the adjacent provinces having high concentrations of factories. The target populations were those who participated in the SIF microcredit programmes. There was also some cooperation with

the Council of Occupational-Related Diseases Patients, an informal organization of workers afflicted with work-related illnesses. 20 of the interviewees had lost their jobs as a result of their illness. Another organization, a saving cooperative in the Bangplee Industrial Zone Estate, was also approached for assistance in the interviews. The majority of the interviews, however, represented the Urban Community Development Network, a Government-NGO partnership.

Of the 250 respondents interviewed in the MCP, 28.4 per cent reported no income drop, 37.2 per cent were in the 0 to 50 per cent income drop group and 34.4 per cent reported income drops of over 50 per cent. For the PWP, 33.6 per cent of the beneficiaries reported no income drops, 28 per cent a drop of less than 50 per cent and 38 per cent a drop of over 50 per cent. Comparing these two programmes, therefore, it appears that the PWP included more persons not really affected by income drops as a result of the crisis.

Examining the beneficiaries by income-drops, it appears that, with regard to the MCP, the number of women beneficiaries largely outnumbered men in all income drop groups. The PWP, on the other hand, had more male beneficiaries, double the number of women. Additionally, in terms of age and education it was observed that the MCP beneficiaries tended to be younger, between 25 and 40 years, and more educated than the beneficiaries in PWP.

In terms of occupation and employment status, the majority of the beneficiaries in the PWP were farmers and labourers. In MCP, the main occupation groups represented are food vendors (65 per cent), labourers and petty traders. Additionally, beneficiaries in the MCP programme represented those who were self-employed and had experienced severe income drops.

In the PWP, one-third of the beneficiaries had lost their jobs but reported no income drop; 45.7 per cent had lost their jobs and experienced an income drop of 0 to 50 per cent and 42.7 per cent who lost their jobs had a drop of income of over 50 per cent. In the MCP, however, 26.7 per cent who had lost their jobs reported no income drops; 20.4 per cent had a drop of income of less than 50 per cent and one-third reported an income drop of over 50 per cent.

In terms of the basic needs situation of the households represented in the programmes, it was found that only 2 to 3 per cent of the beneficiaries of the PWP and the MCP reported that their children were removed from school due to the crisis. Importantly, however about 30 to 40 per cent of the PWP beneficiaries in all income-drop groups reported reduced access to health care and adequate food intake. The percentages were lower for the MCP beneficiaries in this regard.

In the PWP, the average daily income provided by the programme was about 200 to 205 baht. In comparing the average daily working hours between the pre-crisis period and during participation in the programme, a very small variation was observed.

In the MCP, the average amount of credit received by the beneficiaries was between 5,500 to 6,000 baht. The average income derived from the use of credit was between 3,000 to 4,000 baht. The average daily working hours spent on activities financed by credit was around 7 to 8 hours. It has to be noted that the time required for income increases to materialize is between 2 and 3 months. The majority of the beneficiaries, about 80 per cent, reported the ability to repay their loans according to schedule. As for the use of the loans, between 70 and 80 per cent of all the beneficiaries borrowed for the purpose of investing in production. And, in terms of income-drop groups, those with no income drops were inclined to borrow money for consumption purposes while beneficiaries with income drop borrowed money for investing in production.

In the MCP, the percentages of beneficiaries who were sole income earners were higher than in the PWP. 36.1 per cent who reported income drops of over 50 per cent were sole income earners. The average size of households, before and after participating in the programme did not change significantly either among MCP or PWP beneficiaries; the average size of the household was 4 persons. The average number of household members working before or after participating in the programme also did not change significantly for either MCP or PWP.

As for the change in the sources of income, resulting from participation in the programmes, it was found that

- In the PWP, the main sources of income were waged work, self-employed labour and husband/wife's earning. It was also noted that income from child labour remained dominant in rural Thailand regardless of the existence of the PWP programmes;

- In the MCP, the main sources of income were wages from self-employed labour and husband/wife's earnings.

As for complaints on the programmes, 80 per cent of the PWP beneficiaries, with income drops of over 50 per cent, reported problems encountered with the programmes. Of all the income drop groups, the most cited problem related to the short duration of the contract. The second most cited reason was insufficient wages. The problems reported on the MCP, from beneficiaries in all income drop groups, appeared less serious; the main problem cited by all groups was the small size of loans provided.

Beneficiaries were also asked to evaluate their satisfaction with the programmes. Beneficiaries in the PWP, of all income drop groups, rated the programme between "partly successful" to "not successful". Beneficiaries in the MCP, however, evaluated the programme more positively. Between 75 and 80 per cent of the beneficiaries reported that they found the programme "partly successful" and "successful".

2. Field observations

The following observations were made on the two programmes.

1. Public work programmes (PWP)

1. Target groups: The majority of the PWP beneficiaries were male, aged between 40 and 60 years. They were mostly farmers but also engaged in hired labour. Moreover, the massive influx of laid-off workers to the countryside only began in 1999. These retrenched workers were young, between 20 and 30 years of age, many of whom were women displaced from the textile factories. Many complained they had not received any information about the PWP. The PWP, therefore, did not cater for the needs of these displaced workers.

75

2. The timing of the project: The PWP was implemented in June 1999, during the monsoon season. Being a labour-intensive project, requiring a 70 per cent human labour input and a 30 per cent machinery input, and given the type of works selected, it was difficult to assess if the labour targets were achieved and justly remunerated. For instance, it is very difficult to work the grounds during the rainy season whether for foreground dredging, digging wells or constructing earth-filled roads. It appeared that machines were used more often than intended instead of manual labour.

3. As for project management, funds were channelled from the central to the provincial Government, which were then distributed in two ways. First, each village would receive 100,000 baht distributed by the District Administrative Council (DAC). The second way was to allocate 120,000 baht to every district via the DAC, to be spent on any project the community deemed socially beneficial. What appeared to be lacking in these procedures, were transparency and accountability in this process. Moreover, according to the Miyazawa Plan, the money contracted had to be spent as quickly as possible, i.e. before the end 1999. These factors contributed to certain corrupt practices: relatives of DAC members became beneficiaries without following proper procedures, there were more names on the list of beneficiaries than compared to the actual number of workers in a project, some DAC members received commissions, inaccurate reporting, suspicious procurement practices, etc.

4. As for the duration of the project, the period for the PWP was very short and the budget insufficient to sustain employment. Although the PWP generated some positive and useful outputs such as canals, water reservoirs and rural roads, the income generated for beneficiaries was insufficient and could not be sustained. Additionally, beneficiaries of the PWP used their earnings for household consumption more than investment in production.

2. Microcredit programmes

1. Target groups: it appeared that a majority of the beneficiaries were already operating small businesses. SIF funds would help them maintain the business or acquire new machinery or labour. However, with the deepening of the crisis and big firms closing these small businesses suffered from a declining market for their products. The programme, however, did not cater for the many unemployed workers in Bangkok and the peripheral industrial zones who were laid off from the textile and garment industries, many of whom were women. Other retrenched workers who did not benefit from this programme included those suffering from work-related illnesses, again, many of whom were women. From the interviews, it was reported that these retrenched workers had no knowledge of this programme.

2. Loans were disbursed in two ways in the MCP, to groups or to individuals. However, given that one of the main aims of the SIF was to promote community development and civil society, priority was given to group applicants. In reality, however, there were many obstacles and problems in organizing groups. Lack of leadership, commitment, management skills and conditions of the funding were some of the pertinent problems. As such, most of the projects approved by the SIF were individual applications.

3. It was also observed that, as the community grew larger, communal spirit tended to wane. There were cases of conflict in the SIF MCP over accusations of favouritism. In one case, the approval of a project depended on membership in a credit union and this created discontent among those excluded.

4. In the MCP, loans were provided to support income-generating projects but this was not supported with necessary training/skills in management and marketing. This resulted in many cases where loans were used not for investments in production but for household consumption purposes. In some cases, loans were used to repay debts.

5. In order to successfully acquire the loans, clear and well-written project proposals had to be submitted. Many sought the assistance of NGOs to help prepare proposals. This strengthened the working relationship between NGOs and the community, and in turn enhanced development efforts. But there were drawbacks as well. Communities with close and good relationships with NGOs were able to submit several project proposals to both the SIF and the Miyazawa funds.

D. Conclusions

In Thailand, social protection schemes are aimed at assisting those affected by the crisis and other target groups who are either poor, disadvantaged and vulnerable. New, formal social protection programmes in the form of social insurance have also been introduced. Their main target groups are civil servants and employees of state enterprises who are given access to medical insurance and pension schemes. Those who are less protected include contract employees, employees in small firms, people working in the informal economy, farmers, street children and persons with disabilities. They have to rely on self- help, family support, community-based charity programmes, microcredit programmes and government social assistance. It has been observed, however, that such activities and programmes are not adequate and are frequently implemented only after a crisis has occurred. As a result, those vulnerable groups were hardest hit by the financial crisis.

But if social protection programmes are to protect all workers and enterprises from the worst effects of inevitable economic crises, they will need to be guided by a clear understanding of the roles and responsibilities of women. Most social protection programmes are employment based. Women employed in the informal sector, agriculture, or in small, family-run enterprises are usually excluded from unemployment insurance, workers' compensation, and medical or maternity coverage. Retirement income security, including both private pensions and public programmes, is frequently based on workers' pre-retirement earnings or their continuous years of employment. Women's incomes are typically lower than men's, and their working lives are frequently interrupted by family responsibilities.

New regulatory systems have been put into place that should protect against future panics and provide stability to stock markets and banking systems. But future recessions are inevitable. The economic damage these inflict and the human hardship these impose can be minimized but not eliminated. Policies can help protect workers' incomes and family financial security. However, if these policies are to protect workers and families from economic downturns, they will need to reflect basic social realities like the disparate roles women and men occupy in the workforce.

CHAPTER V.

CHINA

Unlike other countries in the region, China managed to avoid the worst of the Asian financial crisis, reflecting lower levels of integration with global financial markets and the greater avoidance of short-term debt. But the slowdown in domestic demand – evident even before the crisis – was aggravated by declining external demand which resulted from the crisis, and by a general loss of investor confidence in the region. Domestic factors were dominant in the economic slowdown and reflected the difficulties of deepening reforms in the critical areas of enterprise and financial sectors, in particular. These processes and the transition from a closed and centrally planned economy to an open market system have placed various population groups at risk of vulnerabilities of sorts. For example, a considerable number of workers in urban areas risk unemployment, as state enterprises no longer provide guaranteed employment and social security to their employees. Additionally, many of the poor are found in rural areas and their source of relief come from social assistance programmes and constrained local resources such as land. Many rural people migrate to cities in search for a better life, yet they are not entitled to the same social welfare benefits such as housing, health care and children's education as city dwellers.

China faces formidable challenges in putting in place social policies which support its transition to a market economy, while maintaining social stability and enhancing equity. The most important agenda item, in this regard, are: i) to provide assistance to laid-off workers from enterprises undergoing restructuring; ii) reform current insurance-based schemes (pensions, health and unemployment); iii) establish a social safety net in urban areas to help the indigent; and iv) continue to fight against absolute poverty in rural areas. This is a long-term agenda, which was not affected by the crisis, but the crisis did complicate China's ability to maintain rapid growth. Important strides were made in many of the other areas mentioned here, and the elements of a social protection programme in urban areas are emerging.

The Government has made significant strides in reforming social security systems. In this process, however, gender roles in the labour market and in the household should be carefully considered. Ensuring the creation of an equitable system of social protection and safety nets to women and men alike is a pressing issue in sustainable development.

This chapter examines the social protection measures, since the reforms in the late 1970s, from a gender perspective and proposes some recommendations for the way ahead.

A. Social impacts of structural adjustments

Unlike many countries in the region, China was protected from the more severe impacts of the Asian financial crisis and maintained a steady growth in the national economy. The country controlled inflation during the initial stage of the Ninth Five-Year Plan (1996-2000) and curbed deflation in the middle and late stages.

However, new groups of vulnerable people have emerged during a more gradual process of economic and social change since the late 1970s. China has been undergoing structural adjustments in urban and rural areas, with an emphasis on the industrial structure. State Owned Enterprises (SOEs) in urban areas, and large and medium-sized SOEs are being moved to adopt the share-holding system and transform their operational mechanisms by listing themselves on the stock market, setting up joint ventures with foreign investors, or holding each other's shares. The restructuring of SOEs has contributed to an increase in urban unemployment as financially strapped companies laid off workers. In 2001, for instance, SOEs laid-off 5.15 million employees, 1.42 million less than the previous year, but a significant number nonetheless. Since the introduction of reforms, workers can be hired as contract labour and are not guaranteed lifetime employment. Meanwhile, there is an increasing percentage of "permanent" workers laid-off as a result of new bankruptcy procedures in the state industrial sector. While the official unemployment rate in 2001 was at 3.6 per cent, overall unemployment rates, according to the Development Research Centre under the State Council, China's factual unemployment rate in urban areas could remain around 10 per cent for a long period (Business Weekly: Jia Heping 06/26/2001).

Since 1978, when China initiated major economic reforms, it has achieved remarkable successes in reducing abject poverty. But poverty still persists, and it is especially significant in urban areas due to labour demand shocks generated by the reforms. Between 1996 and 1998, urban poverty doubled and accounted for three-fourths of the increase in the number of the poor. According to current official figures, the total number of the urban poor in China is about 30 million, which amounts to between 7 and 10 per cent of the total urban population. The urban poor mainly refers to the laid-off workers and the jobless (The Peoples Daily 2001).

With the introduction of the Household Responsibility System in the late 1970s, land reform had contributed to a reduction in rural poverty and enhanced efficiency and growth. But poverty remains today an overwhelmingly rural problem. Official data show that real rural household income growth slowed in 1997 and 1998 to about 4.5 per cent, compared to average increases of about 6.5 per cent in the previous three years. The main reasons include weak domestic demand and the slowdown of economic growth; large declines in farm procurement prices; and significant reductions in off-farm employment opportunities, reflecting both poor performance in the rural industrial sector and rising urban unemployment. In 2002, the number of rural poor, according to official figures, is 30 million (The Peoples Daily 03/11/ 2002).

At the same time, a large number of surplus labourers in the rural areas migrate to the fast-growing urban and coastal areas to seek new employment opportunities. However, many of them are not entitled to the same social security as the urban residents in housing, education and health care, etc. They take up temporary and precarious jobs which city dwellers are reluctant to do.

Women and men experienced the impacts of the adjustment differently. Recent reports have shown that more women than men have been laid off from work. According to one report, the number of female workers retrenched has reached 3,860,000, and this constitutes 57 per cent of the total laid-off workers at the beginning of 2000. From this total number of displaced female workers, about 80 per cent are aged between 31 and 45 years old and have a low level of education (U.S. Department of State 2001). Moreover, women have fewer opportunities to be re-employed in comparison to retrenched male workers and are more marginalized in the labour market. One study found that only 47 per cent of the total unemployed had found new jobs in 2000, and the re-employment rate for women was only 39 per cent (Ru Xin and others 2001).

The limited opportunities for women to earn a living combined with income inequality between the genders have been attributed as reasons why there are more poor women than men in China. Official statistics do not log the number of women in poverty, but experts on women's issues believe women account for more than 60 per cent of China's impoverished population (Xinhua 7/27/2000).

Rural migrants, known as "peasant workers" or Min Gong, are a consequence of China's economic reforms that encouraged the diversion of rural labour into industrial production. Rural migrants, widely put at between 80 and 100 million strong in 1997-1998, are still referred to as a "floating" population. Simply, whilst a household stands to gain very little from extra hours in the fields, ten times as much is likely to be gained by the migration of a family member. But for the household as a whole the most lucrative option is local, off-farm employment. Opportunities for employment of this kind are most likely to arise in coastal provinces since these have the highest concentrations of township and village enterprises. One survey conducted in Henan province found that more than one third of all households had at least one migrant member. Of these, 90 per cent were male, and more than half went into construction work. A survey conducted in Shanghai in 1995, by contrast, found the highest percentage of migrants to be working in restaurants or street trading (28 per cent), followed by manufacturing (24 per cent) and construction (19 per cent), with gender ratios varying distinctly according to occupation. Women accounted for slightly more than half of the migrant jobs in manufacturing and 40 per cent of the jobs in restaurants and trade.

B. Social protection and social safety nets

In the process of the adjustments, the social safety nets system has also experienced a transition from state guaranteed security to social security programmes linked to the market economy. Before the reforms in 1978, the state had provided urban workers in state enterprises with social security, including housing, pensions and medical health care, on the basis of an egalitarian distribution of income. A major feature of the system was the "iron rice bowl" concept for urban state workers. In rural areas, the welfare system was also based on a collective organization of production and distribution. Social welfare was an integral part of economic policy and planning, rather than a separate, residual sector. (Cook, 2000). However, the provision was very much limited, sufficient for sustaining a basic living standard. In general, a minority of urban residents who fell outside the work units system and the majority of the rural population were excluded from social protection.

In response to the 1997 slowdown in domestic demand and in anticipation of declining external demand stemming from the global crisis, the Government adopted a macroeconomic policy mix aimed at stimulating domestic demand while maintaining currency stability. The initial fiscal stimulus package adopted in 1998 was rural based, targeted at areas experiencing the largest temporary shock (the central and western regions), and was primarily made up of labour-intensive public investments in infrastructure (e.g., water conservation, grain storage, road and rail transport, power grids). The investment programme focused on both employing unskilled workers and stimulating employment in the buildings materials sectors, which have excess capacity. Although the package's direct and indirect employment was estimated at about 5 million jobs over the programme's two-year span, the Government's policies still failed to spur demand adequately.

To remedy the weak impact of the 1998 fiscal stimulus package, the Government announced a 30 per cent increase in civil service wages in July 1999. At the same time, living stipends for laid-off workers, unemployment benefits, and minimum living allowances were also increased by 30 per cent, and pension payments by 15 per cent. The composition of the second stimulus package reflected a desire to stimulate urban consumption which has been lacklustre due to increased urban unemployment and job uncertainty following lay-offs from state-owned enterprises, the financial sector and the Government administration. But the large declines in farm procurement prices and declining labour absorption by non-agricultural rural sectors, which were responsible for weakened rural incomes and rural consumption demand, were less amenable to quick fixes.

In dealing with the unemployed, Government attention focused on support for laid-off workers who retained their links to their enterprises. The State Council stipulated in June 1998 that all SOEs with laid-off workers must establish re-employment service centres that provide income support; contribute to life, medical and unemployment insurance and provide training and re-employment services. Eligibility for income support is to be limited to three years, after which workers will be transferred to the unemployment scheme and thereby de-linked completely from their parent enterprises.

While re-employment support systems have been established in the majority of cities, support is constrained by funding shortages, regional disparities and lagging job creation in the tertiary and informal sectors. China places the burden of social protection at the local - mostly municipal-level. Because the unemployment situation is far worse in localities which have neither a robust economy nor fiscal resources, default in social obligations is far more common where the problems are more severe. In 1998, as part of its fiscal stimulus package, the central Government augmented local government funding of social protection pro-grammes aimed at workers laid-off from state enterprises in poorer regions. However, funding has not been on the scale required. As a result, not all laid-off workers eligible for re-employment services and subsistence allowances and not all lower-income urban households eligible for minimum living stipends were receiving them. Reportedly, about 30,000 laid-off workers never received their stipends in 1999, as many local governments were unable to collect sufficient revenue to cover the payments. Arrears had also accumulated in pension payments affecting at least 3.6 million pensioners in 1998. The Government has since made significant strides in reforming social security systems.

Responsibility for social insurance was consolidated in March 1998 under the Ministry of Labour and Social Security (MOLSS), bringing together departments that had been managing urban pension schemes and voluntary rural schemes. MOLSS also brings together pensions, health and unemployment insurance. This consolidation should help resolve issues of unification and expanded coverage, and strengthen fund management and overall system oversight.

The Government's poverty alleviation programmes have focused on designated poor rural areas; they aim to improve infrastructure and provide farmers with basic support and assistance to enhance their income-generating capacity. Fiscal funding for poverty alleviation was increased in 1999 by 6.5 billion yuan to 24.6 billion (2.8 per cent of 1997 Government revenue). While levels of funding may be adequate, there appears to be considerable scope for improving programme effectiveness through better targeting, greater transparency, and closer monitoring of the use of funds.

In June 1999, the State Council issued a decision at the National Education Conference aiming to increase both the quality and capacity of the current education system to enhance human capital investment. To this end, several targets were set by the State Council including: a) to increase Government expenditure on education by 1 per cent annually from 1999 to 2002; b) to emphasize quality-oriented education at all stages of the education system and reform teaching methodology; c) to grant more autonomy to provincial governments in education delivery, enlarge enrolments at the senior secondary and tertiary levels, and implement policies promoting the development of private schools; d) to sustain the National Compulsory Education Programme in poor areas (designed to universalize nine years of compulsory education) after the year 2000. The State Council's initiatives on education reforms were partially driven by the potential expansionary impact of increased education expenditures on GDP, estimated at 0.3 to 1.3 per cent.

Coping with female unemployment

The Government has formulated several special policies and launched projects to tackle increasing unemployment. Additionally, to deal with the new vulnerabilities women face, the Government has undertaken some special policies and measures. In urban areas, the focus is on assistance to laid-off female workers, while in rural areas, the efforts concentrate on poverty alleviation.

The following are some of the policy measures:

- Development of tertiary industry and labour-intensive enterprises as a major channel to generate new jobs for women;

- The "Re-employment Project" to assist retrenched workers to be re-employed as soon as possible; carry out extensive vocational training for the 10 million workers laid-off over the period 1998-2000;

- A major reform of the urban social relief system; since 1995, the Government established three guarantee lines, that of an urban minimum standard of living, the basic needs provision for laid-off personnel and the unemployment insurance fund; by the end of 1999, all cities and counties had established the system of minimum living standards, covering 1.81 million urban residents, including women;

- Salary increment and retirement pay for civil servants and pensions for state-owned enterprises; basic needs provision for laid-off personnel of SOEs, unemployment insurance and the urban minimum standards of living were increased by 30 per cent.

The Government has taken a number of measures to increase employment for women as well as re-employment opportunities, to ensure that women enjoy equal rights. Most of the provinces, autonomous regions and municipalities have formulated preferential policies to promote the re-employment of laid-off female workers. For instance, the Government of Hebei province made a regulation that a subsidy of 1,000 RMB yuan will be provided to the working unit for each laid-off female worker it re-employs by signing a labour contract over one year.

Many social organizations have also become actively involved in the re-employment of female laid-off workers. For instance, the All China Federation of Trade Unions (ACFTU) has provided laid-off workers in difficulties with re-employment advice and services through the setting up of a special fund, a personnel database of laid-off workers in difficulties, job information and training institutions. In 1997, the trade unions made an investigation in 20 provinces, autonomous regions and municipalities on the difficulties of re-employment of laid-off female workers. The study sought out the reasons behind their unemployment and proposed relevant recommendations. Towards the end of 1999, trade unions and various relevant departments carried out job training programmes for 7,890,000 female workers. Up to the end of 2000, the Trade Unions had helped 1,090,000 female laid-off workers to be re-employed (Saunders and Feng Ping 2000).

Another example is the All China Women's Federation's (ACWF) efforts to assist the Government in re-employment projects. The ACWF decided in 1996 to assist one million laid-off female workers in their re-employment efforts during the Ninth Five-Year Plan by way of a women's self-employment campaign. Up to 1998, the ACWF at various levels had directly assisted 470,000 laid-off female workers to find new jobs, and trained 990,000 laid-off female workers. In 1998, the ACWF began a campaign of poverty alleviation with the purpose to help laid-off female workers. In 1999, the ACWF joined with the Ministry of Civil Affairs, the Ministry of Labour and Social Security, the Ministry of Construction, the State Taxation Administration, the State Internal Trade Administration and other relevant departments to conduct the Women Community Service programme, which included the settlement of female laid-off workers.

Birth insurance fund in urban areas

Providing funds for maternity and childcare is part of the ongoing reform of the social security system in China. This constitutes part of necessary means to overcome discrimination against women in labour market. Moreover, infant education institutions and kindergartens are equally important to household welfare and human capital investment.

In 1994, the Ministry of Labour issued the Trial Method for Birth Insurance for employees to deal with the reluctance of firms to employ female workers for reasons of pregnancy. The regulation provided that this insurance fund would be set up collectively by society. Firms are required to pay premiums to social insurance management institutions. Insurance premiums are set at a certain percentage of the employee's salary with a view of setting up the Birth Insurance Fund. The provisions are threefold, i.e. a birth allowance, maternity leave and medical services. According to a report of the Ministry of Labour and Social Security (MOLSS), around 30,000,000 workers joined the insurance by the end of 1999 (Ministry of Labour and Social Security 2001).

Poverty alleviation in rural areas

The Government began its planned, organized and nationwide efforts at poverty alleviation in the mid-1980s by setting up working groups, arranging special funds and formulating specific anti-poverty policies. In 1994, the State Council formulated and began to implement the National Programme for Poverty Relief. The Programme provides for human, material and financial resources to be mobilized to resolve the problem of food and clothing for 80 million poverty-stricken populations in rural areas throughout the nation by end of 2000.

In order to realize the aforementioned strategic objectives, the Government has adopted the following policies and measures:

- To increase financial resources and focus efforts on poverty-stricken areas identified by the states; by 1999, the central Government had allocated 130 billion RMB yuan of poverty-relief finds at an annual increasing rate of 14.2 per cent to poverty-stricken areas.

- To eradicate poverty through various channels such as export of the labour force, cooperation in poverty eradication and microcredit programmes; by the end 2000, approximately 260 people had emigrated and 73 billion yuan of poverty-relief credit was disbursed through 3 billion personal small loans; at the same time, measures to reduce agricultural tax for poverty-stricken households were also adopted.

- To arrange for special soft loans to help poverty-stricken households; special loans at low interest would be provided each year; between 1995 and 1999, the central Government had provided 43.55 billion soft loans.

Additional measures were taken by the Government to facilitate the integration of women in poverty alleviation programmes. First, the Governments at various levels, encouraged women to be active participants in the fight against poverty. For example, in Shanxi province a gender-based poverty-relief programme was set up to develop a statistical system that gives priority to women. In this programme, poverty-relief projects will not be registered unless they also cover women as participants. Second, the Government would ensure that women enjoy equal access to financial resources in the fight against poverty. The State provided access to credit for poor women in rural areas at a nominal sum of 2000 RMB yuan and the loan may be gradually repaid. Almost 2 billion yuan of credit was provided to 1.816 million poor households in 1998. In 1999, 2.98 billion yuan of small credit was provided.

Many social organizations also participated in the implementation of the special programmes for poor women in rural area. The All China Women's Federation (ACWF) for example, began in 1996 the programme "women eradicating poverty" at the national level. The programme was aimed at assisting 1 million poor women to rise out of poverty by the year 2000. By 1998, 580,000 poor women were reached. Another 23.1 million women in rural areas were trained in agricultural technology.

Since 1989, ACWF, jointly with 14 ministries promoted the programme of "learning knowledge and technology, competing achievements and contributions" for women in rural areas. Within a period of 10 years, 120 million women in rural area participated in this programme. In 1996, another training programme – "millions of rural women and 100 new technologies" was launched and implemented as part of the aforementioned programme. The programme trained 10 million women in rural areas; almost 100 million women were trained with applicable technologies; 150 million women participated in long-distance studies; and some 601,000 women earned degrees as agronomists.

Other social organizations, such as the China Population Welfare Fund and the All China Youth Federation (ACYF), had also conducted projects and programmes to motivate women for poverty reduction. Since 1994, the China Family Planning Association and the China Population Welfare Fund have conducted the "project of happiness", which is aimed at helping poor mothers. Other projects include the "project hope", which is focused on helping poor children who had dropped out from school, the "spring bud plan", which focuses on female children who had dropped out of school, and the "fraternity project", which focuses on protecting infants.

In conclusion, therefore, many policies and programmes have been set up to alleviate the adverse impacts of the structural adjustment on women. More recently, the "Chinese Women Development Programme" and the "Chinese Children Development Programme" (2001-2010) have been formally promulgated and put into practice by the State Council. Yet there are gaps to be attended to. First, in rural areas, the schemes and interventions tend to focus on poverty alleviation and enhancing productivity. In the urban areas, the social assistance programmes concentrate on the unemployed, especially female laid-off workers. At the same time, the birth insurance fund in urban areas has been rendered as an indispensable part of the social security system. The gap in social welfare between rural and urban women still exists, with rural women still falling largely outside social safety nets. Second, it is noteworthy that the collaboration of the Government and social organizations is significant in building safety nets for women.

C. A gender evaluation of the social protection and social safety nets

There has been growing sensitization to gender issues in most of the safety nets policies and programmes. Women are increasingly recognised as key participants in society. Many of the programmes have adopted women as a special target group. Women's participation is prioritized in poverty alleviation programmes, and so has women's access to resources.

However, the rationale for integrating women into safety nets is based on the Women in Development (WID) approach. Women's involvement in fighting against poverty in both urban and rural areas is expected to add to programme efficiency. Women are perceived as important human resources that will improve the efficiency of safety net programmes. As such, many social safety net programmes focused on women's role in production and enhancing productivity.

Second, there is an assumption that women will benefit if they participate in a programme. This is not necessarily accurate if women are not allowed, at the same time, to be part of the design and implementation of the programme.

Third, gender issues in social safety nets have been treated as separate programme components and have tended to be isolated from other forms of social security. For example, the maternity and childcare fund is separated from other social security programmes, such as the basic old-age insurance system, the unemployment insurance system, and the basic medical insurance system, in which gender issues are rendered neutral. However, gender issues do matter in these areas as well. In the old-age insurance system, for example, female senior citizens in China – who usually have a longer life span, enjoy fewer pensions in comparison with their male counterparts in urban areas (Peng, 1999). Thus, the seemingly gender-neutral old age insurance system does have an inherent bias against female security.

Finally, there is less consideration of women's status at household and community levels. At the household level, it has usually been assumed that the heads of households (men) represent the interest of the entire household. This assumption overlooks the conflict within household members over access to and control over resources. For instance, households tend to favour boys over girls in the allocation of nutrition and education. Thus, using the household as the basic unit of provision of welfare tends to marginalize its members who have already been marginalized.

There have been some studies on civil society perceptions and assessments on these issues. For example, Sarah Cook (2000) argues that planners and designers usually prioritize programme needs rather than the needs of the poor and the vulnerable when it comes to assessments of policies and programmes. In this regard as well, women's voices are weak and there is a lack of social dialogue on safety nets for women.

D. Conclusions

Integrating gender into social safety nets is important but insufficient. Gender mainstreaming strategies should be designed and implemented at various stages of policy. In order to develop gender-sensitive social safety nets policies and programmes, the following need to be taken into consideration:

- Incorporating the concept of social protection into a macro, meso and micro policy framework;

- Better understanding of the poor and vulnerable, especially poor women's needs and voices, consulting them in policy-making and implementing;

- Paying attention to women and men's different needs, analysing differential impacts posed by structural adjustment or financial crisis;

- Designing long, medium and short term policies for women's safety nets. Long term solutions include the setting up of a well-functioning and equitable social safety net system, ensuring greater access to productive assets, such as land, livestock and credits, ensuring that women's voices are heard in social dialogue and in the participation process;

- Medium and short-term safety nets policies or programmes should meet women's emerging needs around daily life sustenance. Fulfilling some of the needs may not challenge gender relations directly, but set the stage for ongoing transformation;

- Targeting special groups of vulnerable and marginalized women. In the case of China, special concern should be given to poor women in rural areas and female migrant workers;

- The Government and civil society organizations need to collaborate and ensure the creation of an equitable system of social protection for both men and women.

CHAPTER VI.

JAPAN

Japan was not as severely affected by the Asian financial crisis as compared to many other East Asian countries. However, the crisis did affect the country in worsening the economic and social conditions for most individuals and families.

The impact of economic interventions since the 1997/1998 crisis has been very different for men and women. For men, the economic slowdown led to a rise in unemployment particularly amongst the young and the middle aged. For women, it resulted in higher unemployment, as well as a noticeable shift from regular to irregular employment, and a decline in wages and employment security. This underscores the importance of examining the issues from a gender perspective, and calls for policy responses that will address the specific needs of women and men, and younger and older workers.

This chapter discusses social protection measures in response to the economic slowdown in Japan, since the late 1990s. The first part of the chapter examines the implications of the 1997/1998 crisis and the subsequent social impacts. The latter sections will examine the various social protections schemes and an impact assessment in gender terms.

A. Social impacts of the crisis

The Japanese economy which began to show some signs of recovery after over half a decade of slump in 1997 came to an abrupt halt in 1998, and from then on shifted steadily for the worse. As a result, the GDP fell from a modest level of 1 per cent in the fall of 1997 to –1 per cent in the spring of 1998. Thereafter, the negative growth rate continued well into the summer of 1999, making it one of the longest periods of continuous economic slowdown in postwar Japanese history (Economic Planning Agency, 2000).

The decline in economic growth was directly translated into a rise in the unemployment rate and a decline in workers' average household incomes. The overall unemployment rate rose from 3.3 per cent in 1997 to 4.5 per cent in 1999. In gender terms, the male unemployment rate rose from 3.3 to 4.6 per cent, and the female unemployment rate rose from 3.4 to 4.3 per cent during the same period (Economic Planning Agency 2000). For the year 2000, the unemployment rate was 4.9 per cent with the male unemployment rate at 5.2 per cent and the female unemployment rate at 4.6 per cent.

The overall unemployment figures, however, only reveals a cursory picture of labour market conditions. A closer examination shows that young and middle-aged women were more severely affected as compared to women in other age groups and their male counterparts. For example, the absolute unemployment rate for women between the ages of 25 and 26 increased from 15 to 22 per cent between 1995 and 1998, while the figures for women 40 to 54 years of age rose from 21 to 25 per cent during the same period (Nihon Fujin Dantai Rengokai 2000). For younger women, however, the employment problem was not just being laid off from work. They are discriminated against even before they enter the labour market by gender-biased hiring practices. Studies show that after 1997 employers became more preferential in hiring men over women, even though such practices clearly violate the equal employment legislation (Ministry of Labour 1999). Moreover, although the employment rate of new female university graduates was slightly lower than their male counterparts at 64.5 per cent and 66.2 per cent, respectively in 1998, women tend to get hired by smaller companies and for less career focused positions.

The lower unemployment figures for women shown earlier is also misleading because these figures represent only those who were continuing to search for jobs. A significant proportion of unemployed women are discounted from these figures because they are discouraged from formally seeking jobs or because they have been redirected to non-standard jobs such as part-time, contract, on-call, and piecework at home. As shown in tables VI.1 and VI.2 below, women are more likely to be employed in non-standard employment like temporary, day contract, and part-time work, and the number and proportion of women in non-standard employment has increased significantly in recent years.

Table VI.1. Composition of employment type by sex in Japan, 1975-1998

Year	Women				Men			
	Total	*Regular*	*Temporary*	*Day*	*Total*	*Regular*	*Temporary*	*Day*
1975	100.0	85.6	10.0	4.4	100.0	95.0	2.4	2.6
1985	100.0	80.8	15.2	4.0	100.0	94.9	3.0	2.1
1995	100.0	81.8	15.0	3.2	100.0	94.6	3.8	1.6
1998	100.0	80.5	16.3	3.2	100.0	93.9	4.5	1.6

Source: Management and Coordination Agency, *Labour Survey* (Japan, 1999).

  * Regular employees are defined as those who are hired as regular staff and hold indefinite employment terms. Temporary employees are defined as those with more than 1 month but less than a year of employment by contract. Day employees are defined as those who are hired on a day-to-day basis or as temporary workers with less than 1 month of contract.

Table VI.2. Number of people with part-time employment and proportion of women employed on part-time basis, Japan, 1975-1998

Year	Total			Women			
	Total No. of employees (x10,000)	*Part-time workers (x10,000)*	*per cent of employees who are part-timers*	*Total No. of employee (x10,000)*	*Part-time workers (x10,000)*	*Per cent of employees who are part-timers*	*Per cent of all part-time workers (per cent)*
1975	3 556	353	9.9	1 137	198	17.4	56.1
1985	4 231	471	11.1	1 516	333	22.0	70.7
1995	5 161	896	17.4	2 000	632	31.6	70.5
1998	5 261	1 113	21.2	2 073	756	36.5	67.9

Source: Management and Coordination Agency, *Labour Survey* (Japan, 1999).

  * Part-time work is defined as employment of less than 35 hours per week.

In terms of workers' income, the average household wages have also declined since 1997. In 1998, the average workers' wages fell by 1.3 per cent from the previous year, and in 1999, it dropped a further 1.3 per cent (Ministry of Labour 2000; Economic Planning Agency 2000). The decline in wages was particularly noticeable among those engaged in non-standard work. Whereas the wage of regular workers fell by an average of 0.6 per cent, that of part-time workers fell by 1.4 per cent. Since women make up about 68 per cent of all part-time workers, the relatively large wage reduction for part-time workers as compared to regular employees has meant that the impact of the wage reduction was greater on women than on men. The average workers' household income also fell 2.2 per cent in 1998 and by 2.4 per cent in 1999.

For women, the changes in the labour market structure in recent years have led to new opportunities, but also to the worsening of their economic and employment conditions. The deregulation of employment legislation under the flexible market strategy pursued by the Government has led to an expansion in non-standard work such as part-time, contract, and home-based piecework. While these types of jobs have increased the employment opportunities for women, who are often the first to be pushed out from standard formal employment in time of economic slowdowns, these jobs are of little consolation because they are characterized by low wages and insecure employment conditions. Under the new principle of competitive free markets, even the public sector has been laying off their regular employees and replacing them with part-time or contract workers. Research has shown that, since the spring of 2000, almost all of the care workers, including home helpers and care support workers, employed by local governments and other quasi-public social service organizations have been laid off and re-employed by quasi-public and private sector social service organizations as part-time or contract workers. From these same studies it was observed that: 1) almost all the workers who were affected were women; 2) the working conditions of these people have worsened in almost all the cases; 3) the wages have been cut at the same time the work load has increased; and 4) their employment security has been seriously undermined.[1]

Additionally, although the income distribution of Japanese households has been increasing since the beginning of the 1980s, there is a good reason to believe that the recent changes in the labour market structure will contribute further to the widening of income disparity. For example, recent data shows that income disparity, as measured by the Gini coefficient, has risen from 0.35 in 1981 to 0.44 in 1996 (Ministry of Health and Welfare 2000). The National Household Income Survey also shows that the lowest quintile group was hardest hit by the economic slowdown. Their average income fell by 2.2 per cent in real terms in 1998 as compared to the previous year, while that of the second lowest quintile group fell by 1.1 per cent, the middle quintile group by 1.6 per cent, and the highest quintile group by 1.1 per cent (Management and Coordination Agency 1999).

---

[1] The two year research project, "A Survey Research on the Conditions of Care Work in a Marketizing Care Services" *(Shijoka ni Tomonau Kaigorodo no Jittai ni Kansuru Chosa Kenkyu)*, was conducted by five researchers. The project is funded by the Ministry of Education, Scientific Research Grant *(Monbusho Kagakugijutsu Kenkyu)*. Survey interviews were conducted with care workers and employers across the country in 2000. In 2001, the researchers conducted further in-depth interview surveys of care workers' work and their working conditions in two cities in parallel with a supporting agencies' national questionnaire surveys.

B. An assessment of social protection schemes in Japan

Social insurance schemes in Japan provide basic social protection for regular (full time) workers and their families. Of the five social insurance schemes (pension, medical insurance, employment (unemployment) insurance, employee accident insurance, and long term care insurance), pension, medical, and long-term care insurance are compulsory for all citizens, while the employment and employee accident insurance cover only full time regular workers. The social insurance schemes are also occupationally and status segregated and tends to prefer male employees working in large companies.

Most of these social insurance schemes do not directly apply to female workers, workers in the informal sectors, and other vulnerable segments of the society[2] because these categories of workers are often not considered the male primary income earner. Where they are the primary income-earners, as in the case of single mothers, it is still unlikely that they will receive appropriate pension and health care insurance because it is unlikely that they will employed as regular employees in large companies. Moreover, most women work part-time or in other forms of non-regular work; they are not covered by unemployment insurance. For these groups of people, therefore, few social protection schemes exist.

1. The livelihood protection programmes

The main social protection scheme for women, and other vulnerable segments of the society is the Livelihood Protection programme (Seikatsu Hogo). This programme provides an omnibus support, including minimum income and housing support, basic medical care and other forms of care services, and personal and employment counselling to people with low or no income, and who are deemed to be without any form of family support. Even though the Japanese Constitution accords all citizens the legal right to receive the Livelihood Protection if they meet the criteria, in reality only a small fraction of those who are eligible actually receive it.

There are several reasons for this. First, the programme tends to stigmatise the beneficiaries. In fact, the social stigma associated with Livelihood Protection is so negative that most people who are eligible for the scheme do not apply for it. Second, the State is also reluctant to encourage individuals to seek this form of support. Information of this programme is not disseminated and access to it is made difficult. Moreover, for those who do apply, they face many constraints not least of which is the negative attitudes of the welfare officers who process the applications. In reality, therefore, the number of recipients in the

---

[2] In fact, there is a large number foreign workers, most of whom from other East Asian countries, working in the informal sector in Japan. Government data shows that there were a total of 1,354,011 registered foreigners in Japan in 1994, among them 469,761 were working (Ministry of Health and Welfare, 1996). However these figures greatly underestimate the actual number of foreigners working in Japan because many are not formally registered as workers, and many employers do not report the foreign employees in their companies. Foreign workers are often subjected to low pay and seriously bad working conditions. These exploitative employment practices are widespread and Government officials have been criticized for condoning such practices.

Livelihood Protection recipients has been kept extremely low. Data indicates that despite worsening economic conditions only about 0.76 per cent of the population, or 1.5 per cent of all households, were receiving this type of support in 1998 (Ministry of Health and Welfare 2000). Other studies also show that only about 20 per cent to 45 per cent of all the eligible people are actually receiving this form of support (Ishida 1994, Shoji 1999).

The composition of people receiving Livelihood Protection also shows that the elderly, people with disabilities, those without family support and single mothers constitute the majority of the recipients. In 1998, elderly people made up 44.5 per cent of all the Livelihood Protection recipients, while people with disabilities/long-term illnesses and single mother families constituted 39 per cent and 8.2 per cent of all the recipients, respectively. In terms of households, about 4.1 per cent of all elderly households and 10.9 per cent of all single mother families were in receipt of the support in 1998. The gender composition of the Livelihood Protection recipients also showed that women are more likely to become Livelihood Protection recipients (see table VI.3 below). Notably, women in their child rearing years (i.e. between the ages of 20 and 40) and in old age (i.e. over 60) were particularly liable to receive Livelihood Protection as compared to their male counterparts. These circumstances indicate that women are not only more vulnerable, economically, compared to men but that their vulnerability partly stems from their child and family care responsibilities.

Table VI.3. Livelihood protection recipients by age and sex in Japan, 1997

	Total	*Up to 19 years old*	*20-29*	*30-39*	*40-49*	*50-59*	*60-69*	*70 and over*
Total	875 652	147 954	24 001	45 846	101 374	150 386	192 356	213 735
	(100.0)	(16.9)	(2.7)	(5.2)	(11.6)	(17.2)	(22.0)	(24.4)
Men	382 199	74 593	7 963	14 785	45 650	80 504	92 886	65 818
	(43.5)	(50.4)	(33.2)	(32.2)	(45.0)	(53.5)	(48.3)	(30.8)
Women	493 453	73 361	16 038	31 061	55 724	69 882	99 470	147 917
	(56.5)	(49.6)	(66.8)	(67.8)	(55.0)	(46.5)	(51.7)	(69.2)

Source: *White Paper on Social Welfare* (Ministry of Health and Welfare, 1999).

In addition to the Livelihood Protection programme, the other social protection schemes are 1) child allowance, 2) special child rearing allowance, 3) welfare support for single mother families, and 4) welfare support for the elderly and people with disabilities.

2. Child allowance

This is an income maintenance support for low-income families with children under the age of three. The allowance provides 5,000 yen per month per child for the first two children, and 10,000 yen from the third child, up to the age of three. The allowance is based on means income test. Families with an annual income of less than 2.43 million yen (in the case of a family of four) a year are eligible for this support. The amount is extremely small considering that the average household income is about 7 million yen a year (or approximately 600,000 yen per month). In 1998, approximately 2 million families (about 40 per cent of all families with at least one pre-school age child) received the allowance. There has been a proposal by the Government to extend the child allowance as a part of the pro-natal policy to encourage families to have more children. The proposed reform will raise the maximum age for the allowance to 6 years, and will raise the income threshold to enable up to 80 per cent of all families with pre-school age children to qualify for the allowance.

3. Special child rearing allowance

This is an income-tested support aimed at non-widowed single mother families with low income. The amount of the allowance, in 1998, was approximately 42,000 yen per month for a single mother family with one dependent child, and 47,000 yen for those with two dependent children. For those with three or more dependent children, an additional 3,000 yen per child was provided. The maximum household income to qualify for the allowance was 2.04 million yen a year (about 30 per cent that of the average household income) for a single mother family with one dependent child. A total of approximately 630,000 single mother families (approximately 80 per cent of non-widowed single mother families) were in receipt of the allowance. However, since the mid-1980s the Government has been steadily cutting back on this programme. Moreover, over the last decade and a half, the income ceiling to qualify for the allowance has been gradually reduced in order to restrict the number of recipients.

4. Welfare support for single mother families

This support for single mothers consists of : a) income support, b) special low interest loans, c) employment and housing support, and d) special tax exemptions. This income support includes the Livelihood Protection and Special Child Rearing Allowance, Widows' Pension from the National Pension Plan, and Survivors' Pension from the Employee Pension Plan. The amount of the pension depends on the husbands' income before death and on the length of the subscription. Generally, the Survivors' Pension is more generous compared to the Widows' Pension because the Employee Pension Plan provides a higher premium. The special low interest loans for single mothers are provided to start a business or work, for children's education, special occasions such as weddings, funerals, and illness. In recent years, however, the amount of loans provided to single mothers has also been gradually reduced. Studies have shown that most single mothers take the loans in order to pay for their children's education, such as tuition for high school or university. As for the Employment and Housing support, this includes employment counselling, skills training, job search and placement, and preferential placement into public housing. In recent years, the employment support has been strengthened in an effort to link single mothers to the labour market (even though the employment rate of single mothers in Japan is the highest in the OECD, at about 87 per cent).

Additionally, there has been much emphasis on training single mothers to work in care services in the hope that they may be employed by private and quasi-public employers as care workers and home helpers under the Long Term Care Insurance Scheme. The housing support on the other hand has been gradually retrenched, and as a result single mother families have to rely increasingly on private rental arrangements. The tax exemption scheme for single mother families is designed to give widowed and non-widowed single mothers a slightly higher exemption on their income taxes as compared to two-parent families. However, in reality most single mothers are not eligible for this scheme because their average income is well below the basic exemption level. In 1996, for example, the average household income of single mother families was 2.19 million yen, only about 32 per cent of the average household income.

5. Welfare support for the elderly and people with disabilities

This scheme for the elderly and people with disabilities consists of a variety of programmes very similar to those provided to single mother families. It includes: (i) income support such as the National and Employee Pension Plans and the Basic Livelihood Protection; (ii) Special medical and health care services for the low-income elderly and persons with disabilities. The costs of these services are commensurate with income levels and, as such, could be almost free if the income is very low; (iii) Employment support services, which includes a 1.3 per cent hiring quota on people with disabilities in large companies (although many companies get around this legislation by paying the small penalties), setting up special re-employment services for elderly people or those who are forced into early retirement (these services tend to channel older workers into part-time or contract job); (iv) Tax exemptions – these are special tax exemptions similar to that for single mother families but applied to the elderly and people with disabilities. Again, in reality most elderly and people with disabilities are not eligible because their income levels disqualify them from benefiting from this scheme.

6. Emergency social protection measures since 1998

Since 1998, a series of emergency economic measures have been introduced to deal with the labour market and economic problems resulting from the economic slowdown. Two salient features characterize these employment policies. First, they emphasize a deregulation of the labour market. The "Employment Pluralism" scheme (koyo no tayoka) is aimed at removing employment regulations, such as restricting companies from employing more than a certain number of contract (non-standard) employees. With the onset of these employment reforms, companies are frequently replacing their full-time regular workers with part-time, temporary, and contract workers. A second feature of the new employment policies is the emphasis on job creation (particularly in areas such as care work) and job support through financial subsidies to small and medium-size enterprise.

The Emergency Economic Measure (Kinkyu Keizai Taisaku) introduced in November 1998, was designed to save 1 million jobs by providing a combination of subsidies to small and medium enterprises, skills training, employment counselling, job placement, etc. As part of this policy, the Comprehensive Employment Initiative Plan (Koyo Kasseika Sogo Plan) was introduced with an initial funding of 1 trillion yen (approximately US$10 billion at the time) from the Government. The funds were used to: 1) subsidize small and medium enterprises to retain their employees and to hire new employees; 2) subsidize public and quasi-public sector employers to hire part-time and temporary workers; 3) provide employment support to middle aged and young unemployed workers; 4) extend the period of unemployment benefit support for those taking skills training; and 5) to strengthen the counselling, job placement and matching services (Ministry of Labour 1999).

The Emergency Measures on Employment and Industrial Competitiveness (Kinkyu Koyo Taisaku Oyobi Sangyo Kyosoryoku Kyoka Taisaku) enacted in June of 1999 also focused on increasing the employability of unemployed middle-aged workers. As with the Emergency Economic Measures, this policy also provided employment counselling, skills re-training, and job placement and other matching services as well as subsidies to small and medium enterprises to re-employ unemployed workers. The policy was aimed at re-employing 100,000 people between January 1999 and April 2000. There was also a special emphasis on generating employment in care services. During the fiscal year 2000, the policy was aimed at subsidizing up to 10,000 employment and 30,000 training positions for care services alone (Economic Planning Agency 2000).

As discussed earlier, the impacts of formal schemes for women and the vulnerable segments of the society are small. The reasons for this are, first, the social protection schemes such as the Livelihood Protection and Welfare Support for Single Mother Families are targeted to a relatively small proportion of the population who are in actual need of assistance. Second, many of the schemes such as the Livelihood Protection programme are highly stigmatised; the strenuous bureaucratic procedures and moral assessment of welfare officers compounding the difficulties for those most eligible to receive support from this scheme. Finally, in a number of cases, such as the Special Child Rearing Allowance, the Government has also been actively cutting back on the programme expenditure by tightening the eligibility criteria.

It is not difficult, therefore, to conclude that the beneficial impacts of these social protection schemes have not only been limited but also reduced. The impact of the emergency measures to support people affected by the economic downturn has also been very relatively small for women, as most of these measures have focused on supporting male workers who were laid off from regular employment.

7. Civil society assessments of the social protection schemes

Public opinion polls show that most people want the Government to put more effort to solving issues of unemployment, re-vitalizing the economy, and enhancing social protection. For example, the monthly public opinion polls conducted by the Yomiuri newspaper in 1998 showed that the Japanese public steadily rated economic recovery, social security/social welfare as two high priority needs (Yomiuri Shinbun, 1998). Government surveys also show that a majority of the people are feeling less secure about their economic future and are calling for increasing social protection (Prime Minister's Office, 1998; Bank of Japan, 1998). The last few years has also seen growing public pressure to strengthen social safety nets by grassroots groups and academics (Shin'no and Kaneko 2000). All these polls suggest changes to come.

C. Conclusions

Even though the perception was that the Japanese economy was not as severely affected as many other East Asian countries, the Asian financial crisis nevertheless had some social impact on the lives of the people. This suggests that the impact of Asian financial crisis was much more pervasive than initially imagined.

Government responses to the economic slowdown have focused mainly on male workers who have been laid off from formal employment. The main policy responses have been designed to help unemployed workers find re-employment through wage subsidies to small and medium enterprises, and to promote part-time, contract, and other forms of non-standard employment through a deregulation of the labour market. The lack of a gender analysis of the situation is reflected in the social protection and employment policies.

The social protection schemes for women, workers in non-standard work, and other vulnerable segments of society are limited because most of the social insurance schemes do not apply to them directly, and the social protection schemes that are available to them are extremely limited. Recent financial and economic processes clearly indicate that a serious rethinking is necessary if we are to address the growing social and economic insecurities felt by women, and other vulnerable segments of society.

CHAPTER VII.

MALAYSIA

The decade prior to the 1997 financial crisis can be looked upon as a remarkable achievement of the economic and political liberalization package introduced by the Malaysian Government in the mid-1980s. The nation was able to sustain its pace of development, with Gross Domestic Product (GDP) growth rates averaging above 8.0 per cent per annum. The unemployment rate in 1997 was 2.6 per cent, with nearly two million foreign workers employed in the country. The inflation rate was also less than 3 per cent. There were also rapid improvements in poverty alleviation and a restructuring of society as well as in raising the standards of living of all Malaysians. The per capita income in nominal terms increased from Malaysian ringgit (RM) 1,106 in 1970 to RM 9,786 in 1995 (Malaysia 1996: 4-5). With the per capita income increasing significantly, the poverty incidence fell from 17.5 per cent in 1990 to only 6.1 per cent in 1997.

However, despite its strong economic fundamentals, Malaysia still could not completely escape from the destabilizing effects of free capital and currency movements of the 1997/98 financial crisis. As happened elsewhere in the region, the crisis exposed the lack of social protection policies and institutions to protect the poor and vulnerable from loss of livelihoods and income in the wake of such aggregate shocks.

Like most other countries in the region, Malaysia lacks a nationwide social protection system. Formal sector employees are covered by an Employee Provident Fund, which is a contributory pension programme, and by an insurance programme that helps workers who are victims of industrial accidents. But there is no programme that offers minimum income protections against business cycle or other shocks to income.

This chapter examines the social impact of the 1997/98 crisis and the various programmes aimed at poverty alleviation at macro and micro levels in the country in response to the crisis. Special attention is given to the gender dimension of the crisis as well as measures taken to mitigate the shocks.

A. Social impacts of the crisis

1. Employment and job loss

With full employment by the mid-1990s, real income gains increased in Malaysia before 1998. The recession, therefore, came as a shock to an economy that had grown accustomed to plentiful job opportunities and labour shortages. The number of net additional contributors to the Employees Provident Fund (EPF) – an indicator of employment creation/contraction – dropped by 17.5 per cent from January-September 1997 to January-September 1998.

Employment in construction fell most sharply in 1998, while manufacturing, agriculture, as well as financial and business services were also hard hit. In 1998, in manufacturing and construction, the drops in output (–13.7 and –23.0 per cent) considerably exceeded the declines in employment (–4.1 and –7.6 per cent). In contrast, the drop in agricultural employment (–5.4 per cent) exceeded output decline (–4.0 per cent).

In 1998, many jobs were lost in sectors badly hit by the financial crisis: 97,000 in manufacturing, 66,000 in construction, and 11,000 in finance, insurance and business services. The severity of the volatility of employment is underscored by the many jobs created in these same sectors in 1997: 144,000 in manufacturing, 80,000 in construction, and 37,000 in finance, insurance and business services. Agriculture, forestry and fishing also saw employment down by 67,000 in 1998, but other factors unrelated to the crisis had affected the production of and demand for primary commodities. Indeed, agriculture had experienced job losses before and throughout the 1997-1999 period.

While the most devastating impact of the recession was on those who lost their jobs, the recession also adversely impacted others who did not lose their jobs. Wages form a significant proportion of total household incomes. For many households, especially those with low and medium incomes, wages are the principal source of income. In a recession, reductions in economic activity – and consequently, in demand for labour – push wages down. Malaysian labour unions have limited membership and influence, often failing to safeguard workers' wages. While the welfare of the low -income groups may not receive much media coverage or policy attention, their plight is nonetheless real. Most have experienced reduced real incomes because of reduced overtime work opportunities (on which many workers depend for their supplementary incomes), lower nominal wage rates and price inflation, exacerbated by currency depreciation (Ishak and others 1999: 42). More detailed data on wage trends suggest varying impacts of the recession on different sub-sectors owing to different conditions.

According to a report, the average nominal wage per worker increased by 6.4 per cent in the first seven months of 1998, compared with an increase of 11.1 per cent for the corresponding period in 1997. Wage increases in negotiated agreements averaged around 10 per cent during the first seven months of 1998 – compared with 13.1 per cent in 1997. In the manufacturing sector, where 53 per cent of agreements were concluded, average wages grew at a slower rate of 8.4 per cent in 1998 – as against 15.0 per cent in 1997. Overall wage growth in manufacturing slowed down markedly in 1998 to 0.3 per cent, from 8.4 per cent in 1996 and 7.3 per cent in 1997 (Bank Negara Malaysia 1998).

According to official estimates, unemployment in Malaysia rose sharply with the 1998 recession, but did not increase as much as in Indonesia, the Republic of Korea and Thailand. The official unemployment rate for 1998 was 3.2 per cent, compared to 2.6 per cent for 1997 and 2.5 per cent for 1996. These percentages correspond to the estimated increase in unemployed persons, rising from 233,100 in 1997 to 443,200 in 1998. A total of 83,865 retrenchments were officially recorded in Malaysia in 1998, a remarkable 345 per cent rise from 18,863 in 1997 and 7,773 in 1996. However, these figures should be taken with circumspection, since reporting retrenchments only became mandatory from 1 February 1998. These statistics obviously do not include unreported cases of retrenchment, let alone other job losses (e.g. of contract labour) or coercive treatment of employees. Employees have reported (to the Malaysian Trade Union Congress and the Ministry of Human Resources) intimidation and coercion to accept lower wages and heavier work schedules (Ishak and others 1999: 22).

Services also suffered, with workers retrenched from retail and wholesale trade, restaurant and hotel comprising 12.4 per cent of total retrenched workers, and 7.8 per cent from finance, insurance, property and business services. Officially recognized retrenched construction workers came up to only 11.1 per cent of the total number retrenched, probably ignoring the many more contract, casual and foreign workers who lost their jobs.

Overall, labour force participation rates declined from 85.7 to 83.4 per cent for males, from 47.4 to 44.2 per cent for females, and from 67.0 to 64.3 per cent in aggregate terms between 1997 and 1998 respectively. These rates improved in 1999, and continue to rise with economic recovery.

The rise in the official unemployment rate during the crisis was surprisingly small, considering the scale of the downturn, possibly because undocumented workers dominated the most hard-hit sector, construction. The docile labour force generally had no choice but to accept retrenchment, pay cuts and reduced working hours. Pre-crisis full employment and limited Government registration of the unemployed are among the other main reasons why the official unemployment rate in 1998 was not as high as expected.

The majority of workers in the construction sector, which was most devastated by the crisis, were foreigners; approximately 80 per cent of construction workers were believed to be foreign immigrants (Migration News 1998). For 1998, the official data states that 89.2 per cent of the retrenched workers were Malaysian citizens or residents. However, it seems most likely that very few foreign workers who lost their jobs would have registered as unemployed. The total number of foreign workers in Malaysia at the outbreak of the crisis has been estimated to be well over two million. The majority of them are believed to be illegally present in the country, with most remaining undocumented.

The recession caused more households to slip into poverty. The poverty rate increased from 6.1 per cent in 1997 to 7.0 per cent in 1998, reversing the long-standing trend of declining poverty, e.g. from 8.9 per cent in 1995 (Malaysia 1999). Another estimate suggests that the poverty rate rose from 6.7 per cent in 1997 (involving 346,000 households) to 8.0 per cent in 1998 (involving 422,100 households), i.e. the number of impoverished households increased by 22 per cent. Dislocation and dispossession as direct results of the crisis – due to job loss, reduced working hours, inflation, etc. – are estimated to have pushed an additional 53,100 into poverty in urban areas alone. The incidence of hardcore poverty – defined as households receiving less than half the poverty line income – also rose, from 1.2 per cent to 1.7 per cent (Ishak and others 1999: x).

2. Health, education and food security

Rising medical, food and other costs, and the relatively higher expenses and opportunity costs of sending children to school had made education for children of the poor more vulnerable to the crisis and its consequences.

Some aspects of health care have been severely affected by the crisis. There was an increase of 30 per cent in the prices of imported drugs, which comprised 60 per cent of pharmaceutical drugs used in the country. As the prices of medicines increased rapidly, household welfare, especially for the low-income social segments, was adversely affected. An estimated 75 per cent of hospital equipment is imported; hence, the negative impact on health care due to the ringgit depreciation and development spending cutbacks in purchasing or upgrading medical equipment (Abu Bakar 1998: 7). Private hospitals and clinics reported drops of between 15 to 50 per cent in the number of patients seeking treatment. At the same time, the Ministry of Health reported a 10 to 18 per cent increase in patient load of public hospitals and clinics (Haflah and others 1999: 19).

The decline in allocations for public health – despite rising federal health expenditure – and increased health service charges had reduced access of low-income households to affordable health care. Many of those previously able to pay for private medical treatment turned to public services. As a result, various Government health services became overloaded and overcrowded. The relative scarcity of doctors in Government hospitals and clinics – 4,719 compared to 6,051 in private practice – aggravated the pronounced shortage due to under-provision and over-subscription (Haflah and others 1999: 6).

Primary school enrolment was fairly unaffected by the downturn. According to Ministry of Education data, the number of under-enrolled primary schools (i.e. with less than 150 pupils) declined from 1,538 in January 1997 to 1,511 in January 1998 and 1,407 in January 1999; i.e. at the beginning of each school year. Unfortunately, data on dropout rates – which are more reliable (than enrolment rates) in indicating household means for and commitment to schooling – were not available. Other impacts of economic recession on the quality of education are also difficult to identify and assess. Presumably, for instance, reduced learning capability – e.g. due to undernourishment, chronic illness or inadequate facilities – affects the present performance and future prospects of students. Assessment of the impact of recession on education, therefore, has to look beyond enrolment rates. For example, a major financial burden to low-income families, who tend to have larger families, is the cost of buying textbooks.

3. Vulnerable groups

Some mention should be made of certain groups particularly vulnerable to the economic downturn. Unfortunately, systematic information from charitable organizations, affected by declines in donations, is not available on a wide scale. The extent and adequacy of community support – in lieu of adequate state-provided social safety nets – is quite unclear. However, a few groups can be singled out:

1. The elderly, especially those dependent on pension incomes or remittances from family members, including those residing in old folk's homes, face various problems. Surveys suggest that many of the rural elderly have been adversely affected by the lower earnings of and transfers from children or relatives working elsewhere (Ishak and others 1999: 23-24).

2. People with special needs, persons with disabilities and orphans. Organizations that care for these groups seem to be facing dwindling resources.

3. Single-parent households, mostly headed by women, face particular problems and pressures, as mentioned above.

4. Rural farmers, rice cultivators, fishermen and plantation workers are vulnerable to shifts in commodity and food prices, as well as input costs. For instance, tenant rice farmers endured severe cost fluctuations, mainly accruing to rent. For small-scale fishermen, on the other hand, equipment and fuel prices had risen, reducing their net incomes (Ishak and others 1999: 54-56).

4. Gender dimensions

The gender dimension of the social impact of the crisis in Malaysia has yet to be adequately examined. Various reports from women's groups and the media, suggest that, as in other crisis-hit countries, the economic upheaval had a different impact on women and men. Women have been disproportionately hurt by the financial downturn, although evidence is mainly anecdotal or based on micro-surveys. Because of their unequal position in the labour market as secondary income earners and their ascribed roles in society, women were among the first to lose their jobs. Furthermore, women's gross under-representation at decision-making levels makes it more likely that gender-biased dismissal policies will be tolerated. With lower incomes than men, many women feel the greater pain of reduced earnings as a result of the crisis, particularly for female heads of households, sole income earners, and household financial managers. This applies to both women in wage employment as well as self-employed women in the informal sector.

The attainment of full employment in 1995 marked a new milestone in the country's socio-economic progress. The major area of achievement has been the significant and rapid increase of the numbers of women participating in the labour force. This expansion during the seventies and into the eighties is generally attributed to the pull of the manufacturing industry, particularly the growth of the electronics and garment industries, and to the expansion of export processing zones in the 1970s. Industrial expansion has had a profound effect on the pattern of employment and on rural-to-urban migration, and, for the first time, has drawn unprecedented numbers of young, unmarried Malay women from villages to urban factories. While Malaysian women have benefited from increased employment opportunities in the private sector, these have been concentrated in low skill, labour-intensive jobs requiring little job training or previous experience. Consequently, they are most vulnerable to fluctuations in demand.

Following are some pertinent facts on women's labour in Malaysia (CIDA 2001):

- In 1990, the last data available, the adult economic activity rate was less for women than for men, with 42 per cent of women economically active compared to 79 per cent of men;

- In 1998, the female labour force accounted for 38 per cent of the total labour force;

- The labour force participation rate increased from the upper thirties for women between 1970 and 1980 and has remained between 44 and 46 per cent from 1990 to 1995. In 1999, after the regional financial crisis of 1997, 33.8 per cent of employed adults over 15 were women;

- Manufacturing accounts for 27.9 per cent of GDP (1998) and women represent almost 10 per cent of the workers. Major products include electronic components (Malaysia is one of the world's largest exporter of semi-conductor devices), electrical goods, and appliances.

Women's participation in the government sector is important insofar as government is still the single largest employer, although the share of the private sector is rapidly increasing. Women are concentrated in jobs traditionally open to them, such as education services. Also, in sectors such as medical and health services, in general, women still work as nurses rather than as doctors or hospital administrators.

While technological changes in industry have led to changes in skills and knowledge requirements of workers, women are still concentrated more in low-skilled jobs and labour-intensive operations. Similar patterns of gender segregation in the occupational structure persist in both the public and private services sectors, whereby women are not represented to the extent that their male counterparts are at professional and sub-professional levels. However, at the combined professional and technical levels, there are proportionally more women (12.7 per cent) than men (8.4 per cent) due to the size of the health and education sectors and to the preponderance of women in teaching and nursing.

An assessment of the immediate impact of the economic downturn on the labour market showed a marked increase in the retrenchment of workers. The official data show that a total of 46,643 workers were retrenched from July 1997 to June 1998, of whom 60.5 per cent belonged to the manufacturing sector. Women accounted for 38.4 per cent of workers retrenched until May 1998. Newspapers also reported that women were re-employed immediately after being laid-off, but re-enter at a lesser pay or had their working days reduced from 6 to 4 days.

Women accounted for 70 to 80 per cent of the labour force in Malaysian export oriented industries in the 1990s. And, until May 1998, women accounted for 38.4 per cent or 12,853 of the 33,510 workers retrenched as a result of the crisis. Unskilled women workers, particularly women heads of households were made even more vulnerable in the context of increasing unemployment, and the retrenchment of workers. At the time, it was estimated that approximately 18 per cent of Malaysian women were single parents. Combined with low levels of skills, low job levels, and total responsibility for the maintenance of the family, such female-headed households are particularly at risk to lose their jobs, which could severely affect the estimated 630,500 families headed by single mothers. With the loss of jobs, families were forced to cut back on food, education, and other essentials.

B. Social protection and social safety nets

The Government introduced several compensating measures to reduce the negative impact of the economic slowdown on the poor and hardcore poor. One was to retain the original budget allocation for the Programme Pembangunan Rakyat Termiskin (PPRT), or the Development Programme for the Poorest, which is not subjected to budget cuts. In anticipation of a higher incidence of poverty, the Government also allocated an additional budget for the PPRT amounting to RM100 million from a RM1 billion World Bank loan.

PPRT was introduced in 1989 to deal specifically with hardcore poor households and to meet the various needs of different subgroups among the hardcore poor. Poverty reduction programmes through the implementation of PPRT and social programmes gave priority to areas and groups with high incidences of poverty and placed primary emphasis on income-generating projects. These projects focused on the commercial production of cash crops, livestock and fish rearing, some of which were carried out in cooperation with the private sector. To improve the quality of life of the rural poor, the state provided and rehabilitated houses of the hardcore poor with special attention to the design, size and features of the houses.

Other measures included:

- Allocating RM200 million of the World Bank loan to provide microcredit assistance to petty traders and hawkers in urban areas.

- Making smaller cuts to the 1998 budgets of ministries involved in providing the social safety nets, such as the Ministry of Health whose budget was cut by only 12 per cent. This measure also applied to ministries involved in rural development and agriculture where most of the poor are found. In addition, RM200 million of the RM1 billion World Bank loan was allocated for rural infrastructure facilities.

- Allocating from the additional RM7 billion for 1998 development allocation, RM300 million for poverty eradication, RM200 million for rural development and RM350 million for agricultural development.

Similarly, some measures were taken to address the slower employment growth and retrenchment of workers, which worsened hardship faced by poor households. The following measures were recommended to increase opportunities for employment and self-employment:

- Encourage organized and systematic petty trading, farming and setting up of small businesses.

- Institute and provide training schemes for newcomers in petty trading and agricultural activities.

- Revitalize construction and infrastructure projects with multiplier employment effects.

1. Quasi-governmental agencies

Statutory bodies and financial institutions such as PNB, MARA, PERNAS, focused their efforts in promoting Small and Medium Industries or SMIs in the urban sector and credit facilities for rural development programmes. For example, in order to increase the household income of the hardcore poor, the repayment schedule of the Amanah Saham Bumiputera (ASB)-PPRT loan scheme was reviewed and expanded to cover the hardcore poor and Orang Asli (the native Bumiputera). The hardcore poor, with each family obtaining a RM5,000 interest-free loan to participate in the ASB scheme, received the full amount of annual dividends and bonuses. By the end of 1998, a total of RM257 million was paid in dividends and bonuses to the hardcore poor who participated in the scheme.

2. Non-governmental organizations

The programmes of NGOs in particular Amanah Ikhtiar Malaysia (AIM) and the various state-based poverty eradication foundations, also contributed towards increasing the income of hardcore poor households, thereby reducing the incidence of hardcore poverty. Recognizing the effectiveness of AIM in providing loans to the hardcore poor and lifting them out of poverty, the Government provided it with an interest-free loan of RM200 million for disbursement during the New Economic Policy (NEP) period. The loan enabled AIM to expand its activities to Sabah and Sarawak and provide loans to more of the hardcore poor involved in agricultural activities and small businesses.

3. Household / individual

Households and individuals adjusted their consumption patterns according to their budget. On an annual basis, private consumption shrunk by 10 per cent throughout 1998 compared to the figures for 1997. The shift in the household expenditure pattern is partially explained by the substitution of expensive items particularly food with cheaper alternatives, as well as substitution of imported goods by local products.

4. Delivering social safety net programmes

In Malaysia, the "poorest" are households of five members or more with a monthly income of less than RM205 (about US$ 45), or 50 per cent less than the poverty line. A survey by the Ministry of Rural Development revealed that there were at least 114,000 poorest households. The most common factor for their disadvantaged position was the lack of skills and little or no education.

For the hardcore poor, special programmes were implemented through the provision of housing, education and training, income-generating activities, and basic infrastructure facilities. PPRT was introduced in 1989 to deal specifically with hardcore poor households and to meet the varying needs of different subgroups among the hardcore poor. The programme also provided direct welfare assistance. In the rural sector, poverty reduction programmes through the implementation of PPRT focused on the commercial production of cash crops, livestock and fish rearing, some of which were carried out in cooperation with the private sector. The 2000 Budget allocated RM492 million for low cost housing to achieve the target of building 58,600 units of low cost houses.

The Ministry of Rural Development combined with the Ministry of National Unity (particularly KEMAS) also set up motivation programmes aimed at changing the mentality and attitudes of the poorest towards development, before giving them proper training for the various packages of commercial projects under PPRT. These programmes, conducted by Unit Bina Insan (Motivation Unit) of KEMAS, focus mainly on ethics, morality, religion and patriotism. Above all, PPRT has been implemented under the NEP but in the 1990s poverty-alleviation programmes for the poorest have been revised to meet with the challenges of Vision 2020, the year by which Malaysia expects to achieve developed-country status.

The implementation of PPRT was monitored at district levels to allow for efficient and effective management of fund distributions. Beginning in 1991 a nationwide Gerakan Desa Wawasan or GDW (literally translated as Vision Village Movement) was directed towards a second transformation of the rural sector. The movement emphasized the participation of villagers in the planning and implementation of rural development programmes. The objective of the GDW is to involve 3,000 villages by the year 2000, with 642 villages participating each year including the poorest villages. The main objectives of GDW are to develop independent, active participation, empowerment and skills among the people. GDW is also aimed at shifting paradigms, from common perceptions of land ownership and use to an integrated management of corporate rural economic activities.

5. Microcredit facilities (quasi-governmental organizations)

The State together with semi-governmental organizations like PNB, MARA and PERNAS took measures to tackle urban poverty through microcredit facilities made available to the urban poor to assist petty traders and hawkers. RM100 million were allocated for the "Small-Scale Entrepreneur Fund" and another RM150 million to the "Economic Business Group Fund" to assist petty traders, hawkers and small entrepreneurs, including women entrepreneurs, in urban areas. This microcredit fund is meant for the lower income group in urban areas who may suffer a loss or reduction of real income as a result of retrenchment. Microcredit facilities are available for various business activities such as manufacturing, services, transportation and constructions and loans granted are up to RM1,000,000.

6. Microcredit facilities (NGOs)

Amanah Ikhtiar Malaysia (AIM), formerly known as "Projek Ikhtiar" formed in 1986, is the first NGO aimed at poverty alleviation in the country. AIM was set up to assist poor households to lift themselves out of poverty, by providing means of microcredit. AIM is one of the agencies that complement the Government's target of reducing to 0.5 per cent the hardcore poor by the year 2000 in both rural and urban areas. AIM programmes include microcredit financing, human potential development, mobilization of funds, equity investment and economic activities.

The Ikhtiar Loan Scheme (SPI) is a specialized credit delivery system focused exclusively on the poor, whereby credit is literally brought to their doorsteps. This approach ensures that credit is delivered to the target beneficiaries who in turn will be empowered to improve their living conditions. The beneficiaries are poor households, regardless of gender, race or political affiliation, whose monthly incomes do not exceed RM310 or RM67 per capita, while in the case of Sabah and Sarawak, the monthly income not exceeding RM422 or RM86 per capita and RM362 or RM75 per capita respectively.

In order to have an efficient network of credit facilities nationwide, AIM has obtained funds, expertise and technical assistance from its partners particularly the Government, financial institutions, the corporate sector and insurance companies. Through this smart partnership, AIM reached out to 82,218 beneficiaries and its active membership amounted to 57,832 households in July 1999.

The loans provided by AIM may be used to start or expand any type of legitimate income-generating activities of the borrower's choice, according to their experience, skill and capabilities. The major activities are petty trading, agriculture, animal husbandry and fishing.

Under the economic loan scheme, AIM has introduced two additional schemes, namely the Female Single Parents Financing Schemes (SKIT) and Fishermen Financing Scheme (SPIN).

The Female Single Parents Financing Scheme (SKIT) is a financing scheme for the benefit of female single parents living in urban areas. This scheme was introduced in view of the economic and social problems faced by single parents due to divorce or death of the spouse. The purpose is to ensure that the living standard of female single parents does not decline dramatically following these incidents. The maximum amount the first loan is RM10,000 and the maximum amount of second and subsequent loans is RM20,000.

The Fishermen Financing Scheme (SPIN) is a financing scheme targeted at coastal fishermen of Malaysia. This scheme is introduced to help small fishermen increase their livelihood as well as prepare them for the commercialised fishing industry. It also aims at increasingly fish-based food production. The maximum amount the first loan is RM10,000 and the maximum amount of second and subsequent loans is RM20,000.

Besides the aforementioned loan schemes, AIM also provides loan schemes for education and housing.

C. Conclusions

The efficacy of official policies in addressing poverty is difficult to ascertain, though such efforts may well have increased during the economic downturn. Funding for and implementation of immediate aid and crisis-response programmes was generally below expectations. For example, the Fund for Food Programme, which provides low-interest loans to farmers, saw only RM199 million – out of an allocated RM700 million – approved as loans. Similarly, the Special Scheme for Low and Medium Cost Housing approved only RM241 million (out of an available RM2,000 million), while the Small-Scale Entrepreneur Fund approved RM882 million out of an available RM1.5 billion (Haflah et al. 1999: 46). Whatever the reasons, substantial proportions of the credit programme allocations have not been taken up, when they could have generated much needed economic activity or boosted demand.

As the Malaysian economy and rural incomes recovered, poverty declined once again. Many social policy issues still need to be addressed in the long term, in particular, to ensure more egalitarian access to education and health services. Malaysia has made much progress in terms of human development in the last few decades. Health, education and other social indicators continue to show positive trends in spite of the recession. While access to health services is high by developing country standards, and primary schooling is virtually universal, there are growing concerns regarding the quality of education and health services. The ongoing plans to privatise and commercialise tertiary education institutions and health services will have long-term consequences for social welfare, especially in the aftermath of the recession. It is difficult to identify and quantify, with great certainty, the impacts of the 1997-98 crisis on human development.

Regional differences exist in the status of women, particularly between West and East Malaysia, due to differences in historic, ethnic and economic conditions. The Malaysian national framework for addressing women's concerns has been established and is poised to play an increasing role in mainstreaming women's concerns into national development. Overall, Malaysia's commitment to improving the status of women is reflected by its endorsement of international instruments on women's rights and their translation into national policy and action plans. Legislation to improve women's position in the family, community and workplace has been reviewed and amended during the Seventh Malaysia Plan. Outstanding social issues include womens' under-representation at higher levels of employment, and the provision of childcare to support the female labour force.

As with other crisis-affected countries, women have been particularly affected in the work place. The textile and electronic industries, where women employment is concentrated, have undergone higher levels of retrenchment. It is estimated that two thirds of those retrenched in these industries were women. In addition, in their role as home managers responsible for domestic budgeting, women have had to match declining real incomes against fixed needs. This double burden has been met by increasing informal sector labour participation, which has resulted in crowding and lower overall incomes in petty trade and food catering. Female-headed households, which comprise 18 per cent of all households, are vulnerable to rising prices and reduction in income, particularly in the case of young mothers with children.

In order to protect women against gender-based disadvantages, it is important to provide support for skills development for retrenched women workers, skills improvement for low level women workers, entrepreneurship development and access to information on the labour market

REFERENCES

Abu Bakar Suleiman, and others (1998), *Impact of the East Asian Economic Crisis on Health and Health Care: Malaysia's Response,* Asia-Pacific Journal of Public Health 1998, 10 (1): 5-9.

Ahn, Chu-Yub, *Recent Economic Crisis and Part-time Employment in Labor Market: An Analysis of Unemployment after IMF,* in Dea-ill Kim, Chu-Yub Ahn, Jun-Mo Yang, and Kwan-ho Shin (eds.) Economic Crisis and Changes in Unemployment Structure. (The Korea Labor Institute Seoul, 2000).

Bank Negara Malaysia, 1998, *Annual Report,* National Printing Department, Kuala Lumpur.

Becker, G. S., *The Economics of Discrimination.* (Chicago: University of Chicago Press 1965).

Bureau of Economic and Business Affairs, U.S. Department of State, *2000 Country Reports on Economic Policy and Trade Practices,* (March 2001, www.state.gov/documents/organization/1604.pdf).

Businessweek Online, at http://www.businessweek.com/2000/00 30/c3691171.htm (July 24, 2000 issue).

CAW (Center for Asian Women), *Statement read at the workshop on labor at the Interna tional NGO Forum for UNCTAD X,* (Bangkok, 7-8 February 2000).

CAW (Center for Asian Women), *The impact of the Asian financial crisis on women workers,* Paper read at the DAWN-APDC Roundtable Discussion on the Economic, political and social impact the Asian financial crisis on women, (Philippines 8-11 April 1998).

Charoenloet, V., *Study on Implementation of Employment/Income Generating Projects to Alleviate Economic Crisis Impacts in Thailand,* (ESCAP, Bangkok, 2000).

Cho, Soon-Kyung, *Practice of Dismissing Female Workers and Policy Agenda.* (Presidential Special Commission for Women, Seoul, 1999).

Choi, Jay, *Women's Labor, Gender Issues in the Transition to a Knowledge Based Economy Workshop,* (Proceedings, World Bank, 2 March 2000).

CIDA (Canadian International Development Agency), 2001, *Gender profile: Malaysia* (May 2001),http://www.acdi-cida.gc.ca/cida_ind.nsf/8949395286e4d3a58525641300568be1/1dd300712ee37b1485256b490062f1f7?OpenDocument, 15 November 2002).

Connors, Michael Kelly, *Ideological aspects of democratisation in Thailand: mainstreaming localism,* Southeast Asia, Asian Research Centre, (Workshop Papers Series No. 12, Hong Kong, 2001).

Cook, S., *After the Iron Rice Bowl: Extending the Safety Net in China,* (IDS Discussion Paper 377, IDS, University of Sussex, Brighton, UK, 2000).

Cook, S., *Creating Wealth and Welfare: Entrepreneurship and the Development State in Rural China,* (IDS Bulletin, Vol. 30, Number 4, October, IDS, University of Sussex, Brighton, UK. 60-70, 1999).

DAWN-APDC, *DAWN and APDC Statement on the Roundtable Discussion on the Economic, political and social impact of the Asian financial crisis on women,* (Philippines 8-11 April 1998).

Desai, J., *Vietnam Through the Lens of Gender: An Empirical Analysis Using Household Survey Data,* (Unpublished manuscript, 1995).

East Asian 'recovery' leaves the poor sinking, (Oxfam International Briefing Paper, October 1998 at http://caa.org.au/Oxfam/advocacy/eastasiasummary.html).

ECPAT (End Child Prostitution in Asian Tourism), at www.ecpat.net/eng/Ecpat inter/IRC/ articles.asp?articleID=143&NewsID=21, (1998).

ESCAP, 2002, *Sustainable Social Development in a Period of Rapid Globalization: Challenges, Opportunites and Policy Options* (ST/ESCAP/2202).

Frankenberg, Elizabeth, Duncan Thomas, and Kathleen Beegle, *The Real Costs of Indonesia's Economic Crisis: Preliminary Findings from the Indonesia Family Life Surveys,* (RAND, Santa Monica, Ca., 1999).

Gender Issues in Social Security and Social Protection, (International Labour Organization, Geneva, 1998).

Ghosh, *Impact of Globalization on Women: Women and economic liberalization in the Asian and Pacific Region,* Women in Development Discussion Paper Series No. 1, (Bangkok, ESCAP, 1999).

Gordon, N. M. and Morton, T. E., *A Low Mobility Model of Wage Discrimination with Special Reference to Sex Differentials,* (Journal of Economic Theory 7, pp. 241-253, 1974).

Gronau, R., Leisure, *Home Production, and Work:* the *Theory of the Allocation of Time Revisited' in Rural Household Studies in Asia,* H. P. Binswanger, R. E. Evenson, C. A. Florencio, and B. N. F. White (eds). Kent Ridge, (Singapore University Press, 1980).

Halfah Piei, Musalmah Johan, Syarisa Yanti Abubakar, *The Social Impact Of The Asian Crisis: Malaysian Country Paper,* (Malaysian Institute of Economic Research for Asian Development Bank, Manila, July 1999).

Heisei 10-nendo Rodo Hakusho, *1998 White Paper on Labour,* (Tokyo: Ministry of Labour, 1999).

Heisei 11-nendo Kosei Hakusho, *1999 White Paper on Health and Welfare,* (Tokyo: Ministry of Health and Welfare, 2000).

Heisei 11-nendo Rodo Hakusho, *1999 White Paper on Labour,* (Tokyo: Ministry of Labour, 2000).

Horton, S. and D. Mazumdar, *Economic crisis, employment and labour market in East and South-East Asia,* (Paper prepared for World Bank/ILO/Japan Ministry of Labor/Japan Institute of Labor seminar, Tokyo, October 1999).

Indonesia, Consultations With the Poor, Country Synthesis Report, at www.worldbank.org/poverty/voices/ reports/national/Indon1-3.pdf (5 July 2002).

Indonesia: Education in Indonesia, From Crisis to Recovery, (World Bank, 9 December 1999).

Ishak Shari and others, *Social Impact of Financial Crisis: Malaysia, Report submitted to the United Nations Development Programme,* (Kuala Lumpur, 1999).

Ishida, Yoshie "Boshisetai no Kakei to Shotoku *Hosho", Household Income and Income Security of Single-mother Families,* Kokumin Seikatsu Kenkyu, 34:2, (1994).

Jang Ha-jin, at http://www.kwwnet.org/English/data/updatta/south%20globalization.htm, (1998).

Japan, Management and Coordination Agency (1999) *Annual Report of the Family Income and Expenditure Survey, 1998,* (Tokyo: MCA, 1999).

Jia Heping, *Business Weekly* (06/26/2001).

Kamoltrakul, Kamol, *The Asian crisis and its effects on human rights and poverty,* Paper read at the Workshop on Economic Crisis and People's Responses, (Philippines, 9-11 August 1999).

Keizai Kikakucho, *Economic Planning Agency,* Heisei 11-nendo Keizai Hakusho (1999 White Paper on Economics, Tokyo, 2000).

Kim, Dae-Il, *Recent Economic Crisis and Changes in Unemployment Spells,* in Dea-ill Kim, Chu-Yub Ahn, Jun-Mo Yang, and Kwan-ho Shin (eds.), Economic Crisis and Changes in Unemployment Structure, (The Korea Labor Institute. Seoul, 2000).

Kim, Mi Kon, *Basic Livelihood Guarantee System as a Social Safety Net,* National Workshop on Social Safety Nets, (January 19, 2001, Workshop proceedings).

Kim, Tae Hong & Moon Yu Kyung, *The Current Status of Unemployed Women and Policies,* (Korean Women's Development Institute, 1999).

Knowles, J. C., E. M. Pernia, and M. Racelis, *Assessing the Social Impact of the Financial Crisis in Asia: Integrated report,* (Asian Development Bank, 1999).

Krueger, A. O., *The Economics of Discrimination', Journal of Political Economy,* (71, pp. 481-486, 1963).

KWWAU, *Korean Women Workers and Globalization,* (Korean Women Workers Associations United, October 15, 2000 at www.kwwnet.org/engish/data/updata/south%20 globalization.htm).

Kye Woo Lee, *Women in the Korean Labor Market during the Asian Economic Crisis,* (The World Bank and Korea Labor Institute, 2001 at www.kli.re.kr/English/seminar/ session4-1.PDF).

Lim, Joseph, *The effects of globalization and the East Asian crisis on employment of women and men: the Philippine case,* (University of the Philippines, Unpublished, 1999).

Madden, J. F., *The Economics of Sex Discrimination,* (Lexington, Mass.: Heath, Lexington Books, 1975).

Malaysia, *White Paper: Status of the Malaysian Economy,* (Kuala Lumpur: Government of Malaysia 1999).

Malaysia Plan, (National Printing Department, Kuala Lumpur, 1996).

Manning, C. and S. Jayasuria, *Survey of Recent Developments of the Indonesian Economy,* (Bulletin of Indonesian Economic Studies, 32 (2): 3-43, 1996).

Mary Jordan, *Middle Class Plunging Back to Poverty,* (Washington Post, 6 September 1998).

Migration News, http://migration.ucdavis.edu/mn/archive_mn/jan_1998-19mn.html, (Volume 5, Number 1, January 1998).

Mincer, J., *Labour Force Participation of Married Women,* in Aspects of Labour Economics, ed. H. G. Lewis, (Universities-National Bureau Conference Series no. 14. Princeton, N. J.: Princeton University Press, 1962).

Mitigating the Human Impact of the Asian Crisis: The Role of UNDP, (UNDP, 1999).

Moon, H., and Hyehoon Lee, and G. Yoo, *Economic Crisis and Its Social Consequences,* (KDI, 1999).

National Statistical Office (Thailand), *Quarterly Bulletin of Statistics,* (Vol. 45, No. 1-2, March-June 1997).

Nicholas Kristof, *With Asia's Economies Shrinking, Women Are Being Squeezed Out,* (New York Times, June 11, 1998).

Nihon Fujin Dantai Rengokai, Josei Hakusho, *White Paper on Women,* (Tokyo: Horupu Shuppan, 2000).

Ohm, Y. S., *A Survey Analysis on the Social Impacts of the Economic Crisis with Special Emphasis on Unemployment Benefits and Small and Medium-sized Enterprises Finance Programs in Korea,* (ESCAP, 2000).

Pak, Po-Hi, Min, Moon-Hong, & Kang, Young-Sook, *Social Safety Net for the Most Vulnerable Groups in the Republic of Korea,* (UNDP Working Paper Series (II), 1999).

Park, Yeong-Ran, *Challenges for Developing Gender Sensitive Social Welfare Policies in a Knowledge Based Economy in Korea' Gender Issues in the Transition to a Knowledge Based Economy Workshop,* (2 March 2000, Proceedings, World Bank).

Peng Peiyun, *Speech on 1999 International Senior People's Forum,* (Beijing, 1999).

Phongphaichit, Pasuk and Chris Baker, *Thailand's crisis,* (Chiang Mai: Silkworm Books, 2000).

Pongsapich, A., and P. Brimble, *Assessing the Social Impacts of the Financial Crisis in Thailand,* (1999).

Praparpun, Yada, *Small and medium enterprises in Thailand: the effects of trade liberalisation on SMEs and women workers',* in Vivienne Wee (ed.), Trade liberalisation: challenges and opportunities for women in Southeast Asia, (New York: UNIFEM and ENGENDER, pp. 119-128).

Report on Birth Giving Fund, Ministry of Labour and Social Security (MOLSS), Beijing, China.

Report on Protecting Women Workers' Rights, (The Department for Women Workers' Affairs, Beijing, China, 2000).

Rhie, Chol Soon, *Situation of Korean Women Workers' Gender Issues in the Transition to a Knowledge Based Economy Workshop,* March 2, 2000, Proceedings, World Bank, 2000.

Ru Xin, Lu Xueyi, and Shan Tianlun, *Social Blue Book 2001: Analysis and Forecasting of Social Conditions in China,* (Edited by, Beijing: Shehui kexue wenxian chubanshe, 2001).

Saunders, P. and Feng Ping, *Social Security Development in a Context of Economic Reform and Social Change: The Case of the Rural Social Insurance Program in China, presentation at the International Conference on Social Transformations in the Asia Pacific Region,* (University of Wollongong 4-6 December 2000).

Seikatsu Ishiki ni Kansuru Anketo Chosa (Questionnaire Survey on Life Styles), *Bank of Japan,* (Bank of Japan Information Service Department 1998).

Shaki Ishiki ni Kansuru Yoron Chosa, *Public Opinion Poll on Social Attitudes,* (Prime Minister's Office, Tokyo: Naikaku Soridaijin Kanbo Kohoshitsu, 1998).

Shi Zhengxin, *Yellow Book of Social Welfare in China,* (Social Science publish company, Beijing, China, (ed.) 2000).

Shin'no, Naohiko and Kaneko, Masaru, Fukushi Seifu' heno Teigen, *An Advise to the Welfare Government,* (Tokyo: Iwanami Shoken, 2000).

Shoji, Yoko, Sugimura, Hiro, and Fujimura, Masayuki, Hinkon, Fubyodo to Shakai Fukushi, *Poverty, Inequality and Social Welfare,* (Tokyo: Yuhikaku, 1999).

Sigit, H., *Analysis on Results of Survey on Public Work Projects and Micro-Credit Program in Indonesia,* (ESCAP, 2000).

Sigit, H., and S. Surbakti, *Social Impact of the Financial Crisis in Indonesia,* (1999).

SMERU, *Results of a SMERU Team Rapid Assessment of the First Phase of the PDM-DKE Program,* (Monitoring the Social Crisis in Indonesia No. 04/March-April 1999).

Son, Johanna, *SOUTH-EAST ASIA: Sex Industry Thrives, But States Look Away,* (InterPress News Service (IPS) – August 19, 1998 at http://www.aegis.com/news/ips/1998/IP980803.html).

South East Asian Populations in Crisis: Challenges to the Implementation of the ICPD Programme of Action, (December 1998, UNFPA, 1999 at http://www.worldbank.org/eapsocial/library/unfpa199.htm).

Standing, G, *Global Feminisation through Flexible Labour,* (World Development, 17(7) pp. 1077-1095).

The Peoples Daily, (2001 at http://211.147.20.14/chinagate/focus/relief/news/i006/20020220 urban.html).

The Peoples Daily, (03/11/2002, at http://211.147.20.14/chinagate/focus/relief/news/i006/20001007prot.html).

The People's Republic of China Report on the Implementation of the Beijing Declaration and the Platform for Action, (The People's Republic of China (PRC), 2000, Beijing, China.

The Peoples Daily 03/11/2002 at http://211.147.20.14/chinagate/focus/relief/news/i006/20020301unem.html).

UNDP Poverty Report 2000: Overcoming Human Poverty (United Nations publication, Sales No. E.00.III.B.2, UNDP, 2000).

World Bank 2000b, at www.worldbank.org/eapsocial/library/atinc.pdf

World Development Report 2000/2001; Attacking/Poverty Overview, Washington DC, World Bank, 2000a.

Xinhua, 2001, Premier's Report on Outline of New 5-Year Plan at the Fourth Session of the Ninth National People's Congress on March 5, 2001, *www.chinadaily.com.cn/highlights/paper/2001workpaper.html*

Yearbook of Labour Statistics 1998 (Geneva, ILO, 1998).

Yomiuri Shinbun, Teiki Yoron Chosa, *Periodic Opinion Survey,* (April-December 1998).

Annex

Report of the Expert Group Meeting on Social Safety Nets for Women

Economic and Social Commission for Asia and the Pacific

2-4 May 2001
Bangkok

I. ORGANIZATION OF THE MEETING

A. Attendance

1.   The Expert Group Meeting on Social Safety Nets (SSN) for Women, convened by ESCAP, was held at the United Nations Conference Centre in Bangkok from 2-4 May 2001. The meeting was attended by experts from China, India, Indonesia, Japan, the Republic of Korea, Malaysia and Thailand. In addition, representatives of ADB, ILO, UNIFEM, and HOMENET (an international non-governmental organization) attended the meeting.

B. Opening statement

2.   In her opening statement, the Director of the Social Development Division of the ESCAP Secretariat explained that the Expert Group Meeting was part of a broader ESCAP study on "Evaluation of Income/Employment Generating Programmes to Alleviate the Socio-Economic Impact of the Economic Crisis".   Under this programme, social safety nets implemented in Indonesia, the Republic of Korea and Thailand were examined. In particular, the Women in Development Section of the Social Development Division analyzed the social safety nets from a gender perspective. Such an analysis was vital because it provided solid empirical information as to the gender responsiveness of social safety net policies and programmes in Asian countries most affected by the financial crisis.

3.   The Director noted that the Asian financial crisis showed the fragility of the "miracle" economies of Asia, and the inadequate institutional readiness of the countries to shield their countries from external shocks. Thus, vulnerability had intensified and poverty had become more imminent and endemic in the region.

4.   On a positive note, governments of ESCAP member countries took immediate action to install social safety nets for the poor, many of whom were women. Countries suffered varying degrees of shock, and thus applied different social protection policies according to their economic and social conditions, such as public works programmes, microcredit schemes, subsidies for food staples, and unemployment insurance. The questions, however, were: How well did these programmes serve the poor, in particular, women? Were programmes designed with a gender perspective and did programmes benefit women, if at all and how?

5.   The study reviewed the gender impact of the social safety nets. The Director stressed that the Meeting was meant to discuss and validate the findings, and that the insights and recommendations from the deliberations could help define future courses of action, and improve gender sensitivity in the design of social safety nets. She concluded her remarks with the hope that the meeting would lay the ground for shaping a gender-sensitive agenda for extending social protection to the vulnerable – the women and the poor.

C. Election of officers

6.   The meeting elected Ms. Ito Peng, chairperson, and Mr. Herman Haeruman, rapporteur.

D. Adoption of the agenda

7.   The meeting adopted the following agenda:

Opening of the Meeting

1.   Election of officers

2.   Adoption of the Agenda

3.   Presentation of papers:

   a)   Background paper by Ms. Hyehoon Lee

   b)   Country papers

4.   Adoption of the report

8.   Upon adoption of the agenda, the Chief of the Women in Development Section, Social Development Division, ESCAP, presented the tentative programme. She announced that the first plenary session would be held jointly with the regional seminar organized by the Social Policy and Integration of Disadvantaged Groups Section in order to disseminate the findings to a larger forum and maximize synergy between sections of the Social Development Division. Ms. Hyehoon Lee presented her paper to the participants of both meetings.

II. PRESENTATION OF PAPERS

Evaluation and promotion of social safety nets for women affected by the Asian economic crisis

9.   Ms. Hyehoon Lee presented her findings based on three country studies, namely Indonesia, the Republic of Korea and Thailand. She noted that the gender dimension of social safety nets had to be viewed in the context of the overall status of women in Asia. Current data showed that women, compared to men, suffered from under-education and high illiteracy rates, and "unfair" treatment in the labour market.

10.   The status of women in the region deteriorated with the economic crisis as indicated by unemployment rates and income reduction. Lay-offs and, more importantly, underemployment

among women was observed to be have become more frequent. Although the official unemployment rate among women remained lower than men, this does not mean that they were less affected by the crisis. Rather, laid-off female workers accepted lower paid work or swiftly joined the economically inactive population as they were discouraged in the search for new jobs due to lack of opportunities. Further, ESCAP sample surveys conducted in 2000 showed that more Korean females than males reported severe income drops. In Thailand, more females also reported income reduction.

11. Overall, the gender responsiveness of social safety nets varied with the schemes. There were fewer female beneficiaries in public works programme and unemployment insurance. Conversely, in the microcredit schemes, there were more women beneficiaries. The Public Works Programme (PWP) in Indonesia involved male-oriented tasks such as construction, repair, renovation, and maintenance of roads, bridges, and irrigation channels. These tasks would require physical strength and kept women from applying for PWP. Public works programmes in Indonesia had very few female beneficiaries. In the Indonesian study, only 52 beneficiaries out of the total sample of 311 from 32 villages were female.

12. Women's access to social safety nets was constrained by the nature of the tasks in public works programmes that require physical strength, complicated administrative procedures, bias in the selection of beneficiaries by local officials who tended to view women as secondary income earners, and pro-male bias in information dissemination on the SSN. In addition, there were administrative difficulties to include the informal sector – where women were numerous – into the official SSN schemes, and unfavourable labour market practices forcing women to become "economically inactive".

13. Weaknesses in the implementation of SSN could be overcome by improving targeting strategies and designing female-friendly administrative procedures. For example, the Republic of Korea selected computerization service to build up its public database. Given the high education level of women in the Republic of Korea, such a task could benefit more women in public works programme.

14. Unemployment insurance benefits in the Republic of Korea were designed with strict conditions for entitlement which include involuntary termination of employment, active job search, and minimum contribution payment period, in order to prevent work disincentives. But many Korean women were unable to meet these requirements because: (a) women were urged to apply for voluntary retirement; (b) women ceased to search for jobs because of perceived low prospects of finding one; and (c) women were not sufficiently informed about the entitlement conditions of unemployment insurance.[3]

15. SSN policies and programmes could be significantly enhanced with gender perspectives. This could be done at every stage of policy-making including design, administration, evaluation, and the feedback process. It was noted that few women were currently involved in

---

[3] Unemployment insurance was introduced in 1995 and was still in its initial stage at the time of the outbreak of the crisis. A large proportion of workers did not notice not only details of eligibility conditions but also the mere existence of such scheme and their enrolment.

the formulation of SSN policies and programmes which could explain the lack of gender perspectives in some of the existing SSN schemes.

16.   More carefully designed surveys with full emphasis on the gender dimension might lead to more rigorous analyses addressing various issues of gender bias. For instance, interviews with non-participating females to identify why they did not receive the benefit might give rise to valuable insights to resolve passive, or active discrimination against women which had been frequently observed in social safety nets.

17.   Notwithstanding the lack of sex-disaggregated data, trends over time, evidence from sample surveys and qualitative information could aid in establishing gender biases in the labour market. For example, in the manufacturing sector in the Republic of Korea, wage discrepancy was observed among men and women carrying out similar tasks. Likewise, in the manufacturing sector in Thailand, a study found that while men and women in one industry started off having equal pay for equal work, wage discrepancies were observed after 10 years and fewer women were working in the same industry.

18.   It was further pointed out that although comparing wage differences of men and women was important, it was more crucial to address the structural issues in the labour market inducing these differences. The Meeting further noted one structural barrier to be the level of skills – men tend to be skilled labourers and women unskilled. Lack of childcare facilities was deemed another important structural constraint for women in the labour force, often leading to women moving into the informal sector. Poor unionisation of women, due to the fact that women often worked in small businesses, was recognized as another concern.

19.   The Meeting observed that PWP was the type of safety net predominantly used in times of emergency. The limited effectiveness of PWP for women was noted and modifications in the design could make it more female-friendly by including tasks that women could effectively perform, and making the administration and regulation of such programmes more facilitating so that women could participate better.

20.   The Meeting noted that in some countries such as Thailand, community-based safety nets were in place and the implementation of SSNs was decentralized. The Meeting agreed that while decentralization itself was positive, it could involve shifting the burden to civil society. In turn, this could result in an increased burden for women. The Meeting also agreed on the need to include non-economic issues and aspects in social safety nets.

Country Papers

21.   The chairperson reminded the meeting to consider the following issues during the discussion sessions: 1) What safety nets are being implemented in the country and how are the women participating in these safety nets? 2) What are the issues attendant to women's participation in safety nets? What are the constraints to women's participation in SSNs? Are women included by design? 3) What concrete and practical actions can be taken to improve women's participation in the SSNs in the future?

Thailand

22. With the outbreak of the economic crisis, the immediate impact was lay-offs in the construction sector which employed mostly men. Subsequently lay-offs from manufacturing especially the textile and garment industries had led to an increased number of women laid-off compared to men. During the crisis, however, increased employment in commerce was noted. This might indicate the shift of labour force into the informal sector where predominantly women were employed.

23. From the survey of 1,154 workers who were laid-off due to the economic crisis, the majority (70 per cent) said that they would not return to the village. Of the urban unemployed, many were mostly laid off from textile and garment industries. The majority of the lay-offs were married and had children. The immediate impact on the household was a drop in family income, affecting food consumption, loss of welfare and access to health care often increasing the burden of women in the family. Furthermore, women were expected to find income sources during the crisis as they were expected to fulfil the economic role of earning income to feed the family, while carrying domestic burdens at the same time. About 60 per cent of the unemployed did regain new employment: to work in small- and medium-sized enterprises (SME) accepting lower wages, no welfare benefits and the status of temporary workers. Many women went into the informal sector to survive the crisis but the lack of credit, marketing skill and welfare assistance made them very vulnerable.

24. The Meeting examined the assumption that urban female workers were absorbed in rural areas as a result of the economic crisis. It was found that urban migrants who returned to their villages were mostly young. Being unemployed for a considerable period (over a year, in some cases), these migrants returned home with the hope of returning to work in the city when the crisis was over. Therefore, returning to the rural areas was viewed as a temporary measure.

25. Of the urban unemployed and the returning migrants, the majority of the workers affected did not know about the government assistance programme or received no official support.

26. The government crisis programmes, especially the PWP and microcredit programmes (MCP), were found to have failed in capturing the laid-off workers especially women. PWP beneficiaries were predominantly older men in agriculture because the types of work required physical strength. The duration of the project was too short to make a large impact on employment. They were implemented through government bureaucratic structures which had limited capacity to identify target population, had little concrete information and there was little effort in promoting grass-root participation. It also lacked gender-sensitivity.

27. MCP, implemented through the Government Savings Bank with the participation of NGOs, included more women as beneficiaries. MCP beneficiaries appeared to be younger and more educated; it excluded, the urban unemployed women workers who were generally older with low education. However, the amount of loans was considered too small. Furthermore, to create sustainable income-generating projects, funding should be accompanied by skills training, marketing linkages and development of appropriate networks.

28.   A question was raised on the savings level of workers at the time of retrenchment and the extent to which these savings would have carried them through the crisis. The Thailand study showed, however, that 50 per cent of the study sample indicated that their savings were not enough to survive the crisis.

29.   It was pointed out during the meeting that there was a lack of awareness in the family and community on tasks involved in the organization of social safety net programme. Collective action by women at the community level would need understanding of their family as it would interrupt women's domestic responsibilities. In addition, the Meeting recognized the added psychological burden to women during the period when their jobless spouses remained at home while coping with the shock of being unemployed. This problem had not been quantified as yet.

30.   It was also pointed out that the money given through the social safety net scheme was often given as a one-off package deal without appropriate management at local government level. During the crisis, the money given through the scheme to those whose income had dropped were used for investment in production whereas those with no income drop had often spent the loans for consumption purposes, despite the original intention of using it for production. Increasing consumption without production led in some cases to increased indebtedness. For effective use of the money given by the scheme, proper guidance would be needed at the local government level, as lack of information, lack of gender-sensitivity and lack of broad perspectives among local administrators often hindered implementation of the original intention of social safety net schemes. Accordingly, capacity of the administrators at the local government level on social safety nets should be strengthened.

The Meeting recognized the important role of NGOs in implementing social safety nets. NGO-supported projects at community levels were often implemented by women that in turn assisted in bringing gender considerations into the projects.

Although some watch-groups were of the impression that social problems such as trafficking and other physical violence against women and children had increased due to the crisis, quantitative data should be collected to confirm them.

The Meeting also recognized the danger of measures protecting women being abused by the private sector such as the case of job quota for women groups in a school uniform production project in Thailand being taken over by the private sector.

34.   At the end of the session, the chairperson summarized the presentation and discussions. The Thailand country report showed the reality of the economic crisis in terms of its human resource, gender and economic impacts. Lessons learned should be reflected into policy designs especially in respect of capacity building, information dissemination and programme implementation. Commitment of governments was crucial in initiating and implementing social safety net schemes. There was also a need to review schemes other than microcredit to broaden perspectives of social safety nets.

Indonesia

35.   Social safety nets in Indonesia had been implemented in two rounds. The first round was in 1998-1999 and the second round in 1999-2000. The SSN was a rescue programme consisting of five types of economic interventions, namely food subsidy, health support, educational support, employment generation and community funds. At the beginning, the target was the family and it was assumed that the woman was the backbone of the family. Women beneficiaries were found to be in significant numbers in food subsidy, health support and educational support as well as the community funds used for setting up credit schemes.

36.   During the first year of the SSN, there were many implementation problems due to (a) imperfect programme preparation arising from limited time; (b) improper delivery mechanism brought about by inexperience of the institutional machinery; (c) socio-political problems which hampered decision-making; (d) lack of accurate data to serve as solid basis for targeting the poor; and; e) lack of community involvement in programme preparation and implementation.

37.   Women's participation was almost nil on the first round. However, through a community programme seeking to build regional capacity to alleviate the adverse impacts of the crisis, a large number of women participants was noted. The level of female participation varied with the regions; in general, in Aceh and West Sumatra there were more female than male participants.

38.   On the second round, improvements were put into effect, namely: (a) improvements in the database for more accurate area-based targeting; (b) incorporation of gender dimensions; and (c) improved coordination among stakeholders. Women were especially targeted in two schemes: the Urban Employment Generation Programme and the Special Initiative for Unemployed Women. Female participation was set as a performance indicator of SSN and was targeted to reach 20 per cent of the beneficiaries.

39.   An important lesson learned was that public works employment creation schemes would have to be redesigned to include service-type of jobs to encourage more female participation.

40.   Considering that many NGOs in the region had a strong female presence, they could play an important role in bringing gender perspectives into the social safety net schemes and social protection policies.

41.   Interagency cooperation among government agencies was important in ensuring effective implementation of social safety nets. Local administrators had important roles in identifying and reaching the target beneficiaries.

42.   In Indonesia, the rescue package was currently designed by estimating the target beneficiaries on the basis of their incomes as obtained from available data compiled from various sources.

43.   Involvement of the informal sector in SSNs had not been given enough attention by governments, especially at local government level. Only after the formation of a multi-stake holder forum, was some role for the informal sector recognized. The Meeting noted that there was a need to set a results-oriented agenda which could be assessed at an appropriate time.

44.   While the social safety net scheme had been either weak, non-existent or in the process of development in some countries hit by the crisis, these countries tended to lack solid and long-term solutions for the problem. The Meeting recognized the need for building a solid base for social safety nets over the long term. Short-term measures to cope with emergencies could be built along with the long-term solutions. For example, cooperative schemes in Thailand provided various social safety net schemes such as health insurance during the crisis.

45.   There was a need to identify existing organizations/structure, including indigenous schemes, which could be incorporated into the long-term social safety net scheme. In particular, governments should recognize the potential of existing local networks of women's groups as social safety net.

46.   The Indonesian case was a good example of taking a bottom-up approach with the participation of non-governmental organizations. A bottom-up approach could be incorporated in the design and implementation of social safety nets.

Republic of Korea

47.   The Republic of Korea had made rapid progress toward meeting some basic prerequisites for realizing substantive and normative gender equality in recent years. However, the economic crisis had put many of the modest gains made by women in the past several decades at risk. They were laid off from the labour market, and they experienced worsening of working conditions. In 1994, about 38 per cent of working women were in regular employment, while 62 per cent were in casual or temporary positions. By 1999 this had dropped to only 30 per cent in regular jobs and 70 per cent in casual or temporary positions. The feminization of poverty and casualization of employment were two trends that had become more marked with the onset of the Asian financial crisis.

48.   In order to meet the needs of the unemployed women suffering from the impact of the economic crisis, government ministries along with the Presidential Commission on Women's Affairs (currently the Ministry of Gender Equality) and women's NGOs in Korea have taken proactive roles in developing various SSN schemes to respond to the special needs of women.

49.   Social protection measures consisted of (a) active labour market policies to minimize unemployment and create new jobs and (b) protection and support for the unemployed such as speedy job referral, job training and financial support. In addition, policies specifically targeted for women included: the establishment of a reporting system for discriminatory lay-off; participation of females in the retrenchment process; incentives for the employment of female heads of household; establishment of an "equality hotline", inclusion of women-friendly public works schemes; increasing the female ratio in public works and business loans for female heads of households; opening part-time job referral centre, job fairs for women, special job training for female heads of households; expansion of the working women's centres; income assistance for low-income families, loans, social services to prevent family breakdown and childcare support.

50.   The past endeavours to design gender-sensitive social safety nets in Korea have been framed within a Women in Development approach. A lot more work was needed to

mainstream gender issues in order to achieve fundamental changes in social structure and gender equality.

51. In the discussion on the country presentation, the issue of a definition of social safety nets was raised. Although the definition remained as an ongoing debate, social safety nets referred to income maintenance schemes to cope with emergencies. However, the Meeting agreed that the broader issue of social protection needed to be looked into. Western models of social protection had often been the model in this region but it was recognized that there was a need to review such schemes in the context of the level of development in Asian societies.

52. Women's ministries could serve as advocates of social protection to influence the formulation of social safety net policies and programmes, facilitate women's access to social safety net schemes, monitor and keep a close watch over the allocation of resources to ensure that provisions for social safety nets are made and that women benefit from the SSN.

53. It was observed that gender budgeting was emerging to be an arena of engagement for the women's movement.

54. The Meeting noted that the women in politics movement should have a substantive platform. In this regard, issues such as social protection and occupational health and safety could be appropriate areas for advocacy.

55. Governments should support and build upon local initiatives at introducing social protection measures such as community saving schemes and self-help groups at community level, which had played an important role in cushioning the adverse impact of the crisis. Involvement of NGOs in networking and coordination would be vital for the success of such initiatives.

56. It was felt that there should be an institution to support women who were in transition in their labour market status, particularly from being regular wage workers to becoming casual, temporary workers or self-employed and informal sector workers.

57. The Meeting also recognized that the setting up of a proper database was crucial in providing empirical data to convince government officials and ministries.

China

58. Concerns about social security and safety net in China come mainly from the need to deal with different kinds of vulnerability resulting from systemic transitions and structural adjustments. The vulnerable groups of people include laid off workers, jobless people, migrant workers, peasants (especially those living in poverty stricken areas), workers working in some foreign-funded enterprises, private firms, etc.

59. The social security system has been undergoing a transition from state- or enterprise-guaranteed obligation to a market-oriented system. This process affects women and men differently, with the former bearing the main cost of the reform.

60.   Both government and social organizations have designed schemes and programmes to provide social protection for different groups of vulnerable women. In urban areas, social protection measures focused on assistance to female laid-off workers; in rural areas, the efforts concentrated on poverty alleviation. Several specific safety net measures were proposed such as launching the "Re-employment Project", raising the salary and retirement pay for the civil servant and pension for state-owned enterprises; providing preferential policies to the laid-off women workers; providing laid-off workers in difficulties with assistance, including advice and services through the setting up of a special fund, personal file database of the laid-off workers in difficulties, job information and training institutions; setting up infant education institutions and kindergartens to help the employed women; and setting up special working groups, arrange special fund and design poverty relief policies with focus on people in rural areas.

61.   Women were seen as the key players and were the special targets of SSNs and poverty alleviation programs. Their involvement in the fight against poverty had been expected to enhance programme efficiency. Government policies and programmes addressed women's access to resources and finance. However, women's integration into safety nets was based on a Women in Development (WID) approach.

62.   In the effort to develop gender-sensitive safety net policies and programmes, long-, medium- and short-term solutions and strategies for the protection of women were needed. Long-term solutions included setting up a well-functioning and equitable social safety net system, ensuring greater access to productive assets, such as land, livestock and credits, ensuring women's voices are heard in the social dialogue, participation and empowerment of the poor, especially women. Medium and short-term safety net policies or programmes should meet women's emergency needs and target special groups of vulnerable and marginalized women. Government and social organizations needed to collaborate and ensure the creation of an equitable system of social protection and safety nets for women and men alike.

Malaysia

63.   The Asian economic crisis adversely affected female workers as shown in their increasing proportion among retrenched workers. In 1998, 49 per cent of the retrenched workers were female, in 1999, 50 per cent and in 2000, 55 per cent. Retrenchment benefit is an employers' liability and payments are in accordance with the length of service and the calculated daily wage. A total of 23 per cent of employers who retrenched workers defaulted on payments due to financial difficulties leaving the workers unprotected.

64.   The impact of the economic crisis was cushioned by the large number of foreign workers. As the Malaysian economy was experiencing full employment, the "replacement effect" with local workers was not clear and the impact was difficult to assess.

65.   The non-existence of comprehensive social safety nets for the formal and informal sectors is a cause of concern. The inherent inadequacy of protection would adversely affect women resulting in great social and economic consequences.

66.   A policy framework with a multi-pillar approach to protection, taking into account newly-evolving needs and challenges, would ensure an effective foundation for the implementation of social safety nets and social protection measures.

Japan

67.   Compared to other East Asian countries, Japan was not as severely affected by the Asian financial crisis.   Nevertheless, the impacts of the crisis were felt in terms of the worsening of economic and social conditions for most individuals and families. For example, economic growth declined, unemployment rates rose, average household income dropped, and there was a noticeable casualization of labour as seen by a shift from regular to non-regular employment.

68.   The Japanese social security system is composed of occupationally segregrated insurance scheme – pension, health care insurance, unemployment, workers accident insurance and long-term care insurance – and a modicum of social assistance for those who are not directly covered by social insurance. To respond to the worsening economic condition in 1998, the Government introduced emergency economic measures, mainly to assist unemployed male workers. These measures tended to emphasize deregulation of the labour market, and job creation and job support through financial subsidies to small- and medium-sized enterprises.

69.   The lessons from the Japanese experience can be summarized into four points: (a) It calls for a need for more comprehensive regional policy responses, particularly in the area of social safety nets. (b) The gender specific nature of the economic restructuring in Japan points to a need to examine the issues from a gender perspective, and policy responses to address specific needs of women and men, younger and older workers. (c) The lack of gender analysis reflected in the Japanese social protection and employment policies shows weakness in its policy framework and design. (d) The Japanese case reveals the problems associated with a highly gendered welfare regime.

70.   In the discussion after the country presentations on China, Malaysia and Japan, poverty eradication programmes in Malaysia were further explained. Examples were given of land relocation programme which incorporated self-help schemes. Similar schemes had also been implemented in the fields of agriculture and aquaculture through cooperatives.

71.   It was noted that currently there were no safety net and social protection schemes targeting the urban poor in Malaysia. Rural to urban migration and ethnic problems need to be considered in the formulation of social safety net schemes. Existing social security schemes applicable for migrant workers were found to be male-biased because assistance was given to heads of households who were predominantly men. Gender disparity in social security was more marked in the population groups which had a large proportion of female-headed households.

72.   In Malaysia, provident funds which were partially subsidized by employers were compulsory for employees, whereas participation in the same scheme was on a voluntary basis for the self-employed who needed to cover funds entirely by themselves. Participation of the self-employed was thus limited. The system to absorb crisis-hit population in Malaysia, although more developed than some other countries, had to be further refined.

73.   The Meeting further discussed the link between emergency measures in direct response to crisis and basic social security system. In the discussion, the importance of NGOs and other non-governmental sectors was recognized for capacity building and information dis-

semination among target groups. For example, in China, the emergence of women NGOs especially after the Beijing Conference, facilitated the formation of gender-sensitive social safety nets. Prior to this it was noted that NGO-managed social safety net schemes were being operated on a small scale.

74. Although poverty alleviation schemes had been implemented for a long time in many countries in the region, many schemes were hampered during the economic crisis. The Meeting agreed that a different approach for social safety nets would be needed, beyond microcredit schemes, for long-term social protection which would be able to cope with future emergency situations. In this regard, consideration for older persons and indigenous groups should be given.

75. The existence of labour migration in the region indicated the need for protection of migrant workers, especially female migrant workers. It was also noted that social safety nets should be better defined, better targeted and better implemented.

III. REFLECTIONS ON SOCIAL SAFETY NETS

76. Based on the country papers, the expert from India, highlighted a number of points on social safety nets as follows:

- Funds allocated to safety nets are very small and are definitely not enough;

- Decentralized management could improve the resource allocation and management of safety nets.

- Aside from gender, there is an age dimension to social safety nets, unemployment and a range of related issues.

- Most social safety net schemes lack flexibility, which reduce women's participation. For example in India, a simple change of timing in an employment generation scheme was found to have doubled women's participation.

- Part time workers are increasing and the implication of this issue should be addressed.

- Home-based workers are increasing due to Asian financial crisis and increased subcontracting and their situation should be addressed.

- The political economy of the region is changing and there is reason to be optimistic that regional responses to the crisis would emerge.

- Social tensions in the region will lead to greater awareness of workers' protection because it will force government to think about it.

77. Further, she raised several questions that relate to social safety nets: What are the short and long run measures for social protection? What happens to public works after the first round of post-crisis expenditure? Are they sustained?

78. She noted that the backward and forward linkages of safety nets might be crucial in the long run. There is need to look at the consumption side of safety nets. Usually, three things get affected: food access, health services and education.

79. Based on the experiences in India, Bangladesh and Nepal, microcredit serves as a cushion in times of stress and it does improve gender relations. But microcredit does not fundamentally reduce poverty, because its role in increasing productive assets is limited.

80. What is needed is for women to build their asset base. However, most schemes are based on prevailing asset distribution, which tends to be unequal in gender terms. It is important to recognize that asset inequality will affect the implementation of safety net schemes.

81. Safety nets cannot be seen as separate from or just coping with the overall macro policy. There is need to look at how the overall macro policies affect social protection, and to re-orient policies so as to make that a major goal.

82. The representative of the Asian Development Bank shared her thoughts about social protection based on her experience in Mongolia where initiatives were being taken to change social insurance to cover the informal sector and increase access for groups who were not covered by social insurance. Among the issues that she raised was: the need to make macro-policies suitable to the groups that were to be targeted. She also pointed to the danger of community-based approaches in social safety nets as it might increase the workload of women as well as to the limited capacity of ministries to undertake gender analysis. She noted that age was an important variable to be considered in the targeting of groups. She reminded the Meeting of the need to consider the short and long-term aspects of social protection and safety nets.

IV. MAIN CONCLUSIONS AND RECOMMENDATIONS

83. The Meeting recognized that demographic shifts, changes in the labour market structure, shortening economic cycles, emerging social trends and political realities were contributing to increasing vulnerability of the poor and the disadvantaged, especially women in the Asia-Pacific region.

84. Noting the inadequacy of existing social protection systems and drawing from the empirical studies on the evaluation and promotion of social safety nets for women affected by the Asian economic crisis, the Meeting recommended that actions be taken at national and

regional levels toward more effective and adequate provision of social safety nets and social protection.

85.   The Meeting agreed that "social protection" referred to policies and programmes designed to ensure that members of society meet their basic needs such as nutrition, shelter, health care, clean water as well as being protected from life cycle risks such as illness, disability, death in the family, unemployment, and old age "Social safety nets" (SSN) constituted part of social protection to cope with contingencies such as economic crisis, armed conflict and environmental disasters. Social safety net schemes should complement, improve and strengthen existing social protection programmes and contribute to long-term sustainable improved social protection. Social safety nets were meant to be time-bound responses to emergencies and referred to short-term specific programmes addressed at individuals and households who had lost or were at risk of losing or reducing their incomes.

86.   The Meeting underscored that the immediate concern was to enable the poor and the disadvantaged, especially women, to respond through social safety nets, to the emergencies engendered by the Asian economic crisis. The Meeting noted that women had a special role to play in ensuring household and family welfare in times of economic crisis as shown by the experience during the Asian financial crisis of 1997. Thus, the consideration of social safety nets should take into full account the significant role of women in coping with the adverse impacts of the economic crisis. In the selection of SSN programmes, special attention should be given to the appropriateness of the programme to address gender issues.

I. Policies

87.   The Meeting affirmed that social protection was a human right and that every citizen was entitled to minimum basic services such as access to food, health, and education. Governments and international organizations had introduced several programmes as social safety nets to fulfil this obligation. Economic crises highlighted inadequacies in these programmes. The Meeting found that some failures were attributable to such factors as: (a) inconsistencies between macroeconomic policies and social protection goals whereby the former undermined the effectiveness of the latter; (b) inadequate/insufficient financial resources and political commitment; (c) failures in information dissemination about the schemes and in reaching out to the intended target population; (d) vague criteria used in identifying target groups, such as not specifying gender and age dimensions; and (e) exclusion of stakeholders from designing and evaluating the schemes.

Successfully assisting women in vulnerable conditions, through social safety nets, requires political will and commitment, especially to social and gender issues. The Meeting noted that lack of strong political will or commitment was salient in the cases where schemes did not work and this was clearly shown in the inadequacy of funding. Other relevant issues were gender bias within the government machinery and policy-making, inadequate attention to local and/or changing socio-economic conditions, closed decision-making within the bureaucracy that excluded civil society or target populations from participating in project design and implementation.

Recommendations

88.   Conscious efforts should be taken to ensure long-term sustainability and to eliminate inconsistencies between macro-policies and social protection goals. Such inconsistencies can lead to outcomes whereby safety net programs are undermined by the processes set into motion by macro-policies such as trade liberalization and fiscal cutbacks.

89.   Budget allocation should be reoriented toward pro-poor policy implementation and expanding the resource base for social safety nets.

90.   Macro-policies should be redirected toward the provision of basic needs and services, with special attention to the needs of women. Macro-policies that conflict with these social objectives need to be reconsidered.

91.   There should be deliberate efforts to take into account gender and age dimensions in social protection as well as asset distribution. Emerging realities in the labour market structure as reflected by casualization and informalization should be recognized and addressed in social protection policies.

92.   Gender auditing of social protection and safety net schemes as well as all government policies should be undertaken. In this regard, gender focal points in government should be trained in gender auditing.

93.   Considering the existence of labour migration, especially female migration, within the region, the need for social protection among migrant workers is recognized. There is a need to provide and facilitate access to social protection and safety nets for migrant workers in the host countries and this may require regional agreements and/or enforcement of existing agreements among sending and host countries.

94.   Social safety net programmes, especially microcredit schemes, should be re-oriented toward asset building and value-adding economic activities in order to maximize its benefits and ensure long-term income flows and sustainability.

95.   The formulation and adoption of gender-responsive social protection and safety net policies could be included in the platform of women leaders and politicians and those seeking to promote female participation in politics, decision- making and governance.

96.   The role of women's ministries should not be confined to specific women's projects but should include gender mainstreaming in all policies and programmes, including social safety nets policies and programmes administered by other ministries. Women's ministries could advocate for the design and implementation of gender-responsive social safety nets and social protection policies and programmes as well as the channelling of gender budgets (where they exist) and national resources to SSNs, among the relevant agencies of government.

II. Stakeholders participation

97.   The Meeting found that in implementing social safety net schemes, countries had taken several improvement measures in terms of addressing the needs of women, including the formation of multi-stakeholder mechanisms. These mechanisms enabled the schemes to better involve and coordinate the informal sector of which the majority was often women. The participation of multi-stakeholders often resulted in better utilization of existing NGOs that had worked for women's interests and facilitated such areas as consultation with prospective beneficiaries and implementation of community-based microcredit programmes thus helping to incorporate gender considerations into the programmes. The Meeting also found that indigenous groups and existing community-based organizations had helped to cushion the impact of the economic crisis. The Meeting noted these lessons should be incorporated in future projects so that social safety nets could fully serve the intended targets, including those employed in the informal sector, home-based workers, part-time workers, older workers as well as those who would have to prioritize caring for the family over paid work.

Recommendations

98.   Governmental and non-governmental organizations have mutually supportive and complementary roles to play in the effective provision of social safety nets. NGOs and other stakeholders should be encouraged to participate in designing, implementing and evaluating social safety nets schemes. Prospective participants in such endeavour should be given adequate training in the formulation of gender-sensitive social protection and safety net policies and programmes as well as in communication and information dissemination. Project monitoring should include mechanisms for ensuring accountability of NGOs involved in the delivery of safety nets and social protection measures.

99.   Mechanisms should be established for social dialogue and consultation among stakeholders on social protection and safety net policies, including strengthening the working relationship between governments and non-governmental organizations in the design and implementation of social safety nets and social protection policies and programmes.

100.   Greater scope should be allowed for social movements and organizations, especially of women, to push gender-sensitive policies.

101.   Efforts should be made to increase women's representation in governments, including local governments and encourage them to advocate for the adoption of gender-sensitive safety nets and social protection policies and programmes.

102.   Greater devolution should be promoted of financial and other powers from central government to locally accountable bodies that could effectively assist in the delivery of social safety nets and social protection measures.

103.   The participation of local organizations – governmental and non-governmental – in the design, implementation and monitoring of the impacts of social protection and safety net programmes should be encouraged to ensure efficacy and gender responsiveness.

104.   Measures should be taken to ensure the sustainability of social protection programmes and the accountability of NGOs involved in the delivery of social safety nets.

III. Modalities of implementation

105.   The Meeting found that several deficiencies in existing methods of data collection and in database management had impeded development of social safety nets policies and programmes which had to be based on the realities and needs of the target population. The Meeting noted that the lack of standardization of key concepts, such as "social protection" and "safety nets", hindered the establishment of comparability of data across countries. The dearth of accurate and reliable sex-disaggregated data, especially at the meso- and micro-levels, was found to have obstructed analysis of gender impacts of crisis and of social safety nets. The need to supplement such data with qualitative data, such as on women's perceptions and how they cope with the crisis was acknowledged, as qualitative and quantitative data could together enable comprehensive analyses of gender issues that pertain to social protection and safety nets, such as divorce rates, and violence against women. The lack of access to databases, especially the data collected by national authorities, was found to be an added constraint.

Recommendations

106.   Regional and international organizations such as ESCAP, the ADB, and the World Bank could facilitate and/or support the coordination of the compilation of existing data on social protection, safety nets, and gender at the national level. This could be done through technical assistance programmes to women's ministries, labour and social welfare agencies, national statistical offices and should take into account the demand of users of such data including policy makers, implementers/administrators and non-governmental organizations.

107.   ESCAP should continue to organize the exchange of information and expand its work in the field of social protection and safety nets. This should include the documentation of case studies on community-based and indigenous social protection schemes, and publication and dissemination of such information.

108.   Regular, accurate and reliable sex-disaggregated data that are vital in formulating social protection and safety net policies and analysing their gender impacts should be compiled. This should include the development of appropriate analytical frameworks and social indicators for more methodologically rigorous analysis and that would facilitate better targeting, better definition and implementation of SSN policies and programmes.

109.   Awareness of national statisticians should be raised on the importance of data on social protection and safety nets and its link to gender issues as well as its implications for policy-making and evaluation of the gender impacts of policies. This could be done through technical assistance programmes.

110.   The standardization of concepts and statistics as well as the conduct of qualitative studies pertaining to social protection and safety nets and its gender dimensions. (i.e. divorce, violence against women, etc.) should be encouraged.

111.   There is a need to improve targeting beneficiaries and reduce leakage in the implementation of social safety nets. Criteria for eligibility should be carefully thought out. Local level organizations, especially women's organizations, could assist in identifying individuals. There should be more deliberate efforts to include women, especially in social safety nets that have built-in male biases such as public works programmes.

112.   Measures should be taken to support effective safety net programmes and build upon successful community-based and indigenous schemes that are in place and to ensure that policies would not undermine such programmes.

113.   Social protection policies and safety net schemes that are flexible enough to allow for local interpretation and adaptation over time and that would accommodate the needs and circumstances of women should be developed.

114.   Information on social safety nets should be properly disseminated to the target groups, especially women.

115.   Efforts should be made to raise awareness on the need for gender-responsive social safety net policies and to build the capacity of government and non-governmental organizations in the design and implementation of gender-sensitive measures for social protection and safety nets.